D0803353

THE IKEA EDGE

Building Global Growth and Social Good at the World's Most Iconic Home Store

ANDERS DAHLVIG

New York   Chicago   San Francisco   Lisbon   London   Madrid   Mexico City
Milan   New Delhi   San Juan   Seoul   Singapore   Sydney   Toronto

1 2 3 4 5 6 7 8 9 10 QFR/QFR 1 6 5 4 3 2 1

ISBN   978-0-07-177765-0
MHID   0-07-177765-2

e-ISBN 978-0-07-177764-3
e-MHID   0-07-177764-4

Library of Congress Cataloging-in-Publication Data
Dahlvig, Anders.
   The IKEA edge : building global growth and social good at the world's most iconic home store / by
Anders Dahlvig.
      p. cm.
   ISBN-13: 978-0-07-177765-0 (alk. paper)
   ISBN-10: 0-07-177765-2 (alk. paper)
   1. Ikea (Firm) 2. Furniture industry and trade—Sweden—Management.
3. Social responsibility of
business—Sweden. I. Title.
   HD9773.S84I453 2012
   658—dc23

                                                                                        2011032233

McGraw-Hill books are available at special quantity discounts to use as premiums and sales promotions or for use in corporate training programs. To contact a representative, please e-mail us at bulksales@mcgraw-hill.com.

This book is printed on acid-free paper.

To my many friends and colleagues at Ikea.
You are the company's biggest secret of success.

Contents

Prologue

I t wasn't my last day at Ikea but it felt that way.

The Swedish summer morning at the end of June 2009 was perfect. We had just finished spending two days with the 300 top managers of Ikea, going through the new five-year plan that was to succeed our plan for the past 10 years. A fantastic goodbye party had been arranged the evening before. It was a very emotional time for me and many of my friends—a moment that will remain as one of my best memories.

I had one more task before I left Älmhult for the last time as an Ikea employee: my final Webcast for the monthly editorial on the Ikea website. It so happened that this took place in the "old HQ" in Älmhult, the town where Ikea started its business 65 years ago. This building had once been the headquarters for Ikea and had kept that name ever since. This was the very building where I had my first interview before joining the company 26 years earlier.

Stepping into the reception area, I noticed that it looked almost exactly the same as it had back then. The shoot took place in the basement with a small video camera. A piece of green paper was put on the wall behind me to cover the concrete. There were no fancy studios or external media company. After finishing, I passed Bosse Franzen, a longtime Ikea employee who was editing the second part of the Ikea history DVD in his little basement office. He invited me to look at a couple of pieces from the movie. We sat together, reflecting on our experiences with the company.

The process to find my successor had been going on for some time. When I took the job of CEO in 1999, I had said to Ingvar Kamprad, the founder of Ikea, that 10 years seemed to be a good length of time to remain in the position—provided, of course, that I did the job well. With that sentiment in mind, our guiding document had been a 10-year direction. Now, approaching the end of the decade, it still felt right to leave. I recounted the reasons:

- We needed a new long-term plan.
- The sons of the founder were getting more involved in the company and with the board.
- I was starting to lose the drive and energy needed for the job.
- It was good for Ikea to make the change, and it was good for me too. I wanted to spend more time with my sons before they left school.
- There was a new manager for the company, one with new ideas and energy. He was connected to and recruited by the new board. It felt like a natural point to make the break.

I was happy with the choice of my successor. Mikael Ohlsson was a very experienced and well-liked Ikea colleague. He had been part of the management team for many years and stood behind the plans going forward. In fact, he'd been heavily involved in developing them. Some healthy change was needed, and he projected an aura of security, continuity, and stability in his succession. That was something many Ikea colleagues would appreciate.

Many seemed surprised I wasn't planning to stay on at the company in another role. That sentiment says a lot about Ikea. "Why would anyone want to work somewhere else?" they wondered. Occasionally I pondered the same thing. Was I really making the right decision? I was sure we could have worked out a new role for me.

On reflection, though, I knew I was right. It was time for a new chapter in my life. My plan was to take on nonexecutive roles on different companies' boards. I wanted to have more time for my family, and I wanted to be my own boss. I also wanted to see how my experience could benefit other businesses and learn from them in a new role. Above all, I wanted to apply the lessons I'd learned from working at Ikea. *And now, as I exited through the doors, I wondered how I would do that.*

Introduction

I am a true believer in capitalism and an open and free global economy. The business community is perhaps the most important contributor to generating growth, prosperity, and finding solutions to the big challenges of our planet—poverty and the environmental dangers we are facing. All of my years in business have reinforced this idea. Public advocacy groups certainly have an important role to play in this process, but I believe business's participation in these concerns is essential.

It is thus with growing concern that I note what seems to be an increasing divide between business and the general public. Almost every day, there are reports in the media about company malpractices, greed, or even outright criminal behavior. The most evident examples are probably companies in the finance sector in countries like the United States, UK, and Ireland, and companies linked to various environmental disasters. Among the names that come to mind are WorldCom, Enron, BP, Exxon, and Bernard Madoff. But no one runs a business free from scrutiny. The respect for and trust of the business community is at risk.

Why is this happening? With the rise of the Internet, extended legislation, and the evolution of media, the transparency of companies has increased enormously. Company practices are not necessarily any worse than before—probably the contrary—but today nothing can be hidden from the public.

The demands people put on business have also changed. It is no longer enough to pay taxes and create jobs. Companies are expected to take a much broader role in society. They should improve standards at suppliers (both environmental and working conditions), encourage diversity in the workforce, offer better pay and conditions for their own employees, help with integration of minorities in the society, find solutions to environmental threats, support democracy, and work actively against corruption.

The Purpose of Business

What about the point of view of the business community? Have businesses moved with the times? Probably not enough, or we would not see such massive critical scrutiny from the media and authorities. Is this simply a problem of the moral and ethical standings of individual managers? Or is it the result of an outdated system—legislation, company structures, and governance? Are managers today pressured more than in the past for results and capabilities (or lack of them), or has the purpose of business evolved fundamentally? Perhaps that is at the core of the lack of trust in business among many people and institutions.

Should the overriding purpose of the corporate community be to maximize shareholder (and managers') wealth, as seems to be the predominant view within the business community? Or should business contribute in a more substantial way to a better world? Basically, it all comes down to whether the profit motive of business can be reconciled with the broader interests of society.

Can the trend be reversed, and can society return to the old idea that "the business of business is business," as the old saying goes? The chances of that occurring are slim. In fact, precisely the opposite seems to be the case. The growing gap between rich and poor in many Western countries, the slow progress in eradicating poverty in many developing countries, the increasing danger of environmental disasters—all of these realities speak to a continued pressure on business to take a larger role in developing our society. Until the business community aligns its views regarding its purpose, different stakeholders such as unions, NGOs, and the media will continue to exert pressure for change. It's time for the business community to take the initiative ourselves and determine what's best for ourselves.

Giving Back to Society

What does it mean to contribute in a bigger way to a better society? Most companies define their fundamental mission as maximizing shareholder wealth. If they do this, so the argument goes, they will create jobs, pay taxes, and thus contribute to society. To show good intentions, some companies tack on social and environmental work. But no one loses sight of the fact that the priority is to make the shareholders—and often also the management—wealthier. As the author Charles Handy so nicely put it, "Capitalism depends on people working terribly hard to make other people rich, in the hope, often misplaced, that they will get rich themselves. Growth depends on making people envious of other people so that they want what the others have."

To me this seems like a very empty life. *As a result of my many years at Ikea and through the development of my personal values system, I've come to believe most people feel motivated and happy if work has a bigger meaning beyond power, wealth, and other inflated statements.* The work we do in business should create *lasting value* and do good for others. This is not a semantic quibble; it is a serious moral point.

Contributing to a better society can mean many things, but it should include a more balanced approach in considering all stakeholders of the company—shareholders, employees, customers, suppliers, suppliers' employees, the community, and society at large. Beyond simply returning enhanced value to shareholders, companies should also set bigger objectives, such as helping to reduce poverty, create a better environment, or promote more equality.

When a company is seen to harbor genuine ambitions such as these, it attracts the best people—those who want to work for something more than a paycheck. Staffing a company with the best people is key to achieving the best business results (i.e., profit). In this way, enhanced social responsibility will also lead to happy shareholders.

We can endlessly debate which is the chicken and which is the egg in this scenario, but the point is that contributing to a better society and the old-fashioned business objectives as we know them today (maximizing shareholders' wealth) can be accomplished simultaneously. Indeed, they are dependent upon one another.

What Are the Trade-Offs?

Skeptics will say there must be a trade-off—some conflicts of interest that will work to the disadvantage of shareholders. It's true that such apparent conflicts will arise. The challenge in understanding and resolving them is that potential "extra" costs or investments often are up front and already visible. Benefits, on the other hand— the results produced by motivated and skilled employees, loyal customers, better supplier relationships, more favorable media coverage, etc.—are more visible over the long term and therefore difficult to quantify financially. *The more long term your business perspective is, the more likely you are to see the benefits of your commitment to society also in monetary terms.*

During my 26 years with Ikea, I never felt any doubt that the company had genuinely good intentions. Like any business, Ikea strove for professionalism and profits. But this was never an end in itself. The company has a social ambition that feels genuine: to create a better everyday life for people. Today it is my conviction that this overarching ambition together with responsible management practices is the reason for the company's achievements.

Consider this about Ikea:

* During 1999–2009, yearly average sales growth was 11 percent.
* Operating profit was well over 10 percent of sales every year.
* Sales prices were reduced by 20 percent.
* The company added 70,000 to its workforce.

At the same time, in various rankings Ikea is well placed on brand recognition and innovation and corporate social responsibility (CSR), and it is an employer of choice.

I don't want to suggest that Ikea is a perfect company in every respect. The point is that Ikea's experience shows it's possible to combine good business results with being a good citizen and to gain the trust of the general public.

The Purpose of This Book

The purpose of this book is not to tell the story of Ikea. Instead, my intention is to use Ikea as an example of good corporate citizenship. I want to establish some of the prerequisites for a business that has the ambition to achieve both traditional business goals such as profit and sales growth and to contribute to a better society. Maybe in some small way this will help more companies broaden their perspective. And when they do that, people's trust in business will improve.

Also, this is not a book about Ikea's founder, Ingvar Kamprad, though much of his philosophical approach runs through my work. Kamprad is extremely important to Ikea, but much has already been written about him, and I don't think I can add very much to what has already been said. This is also not a book about Anders Dahlvig. Nor is this a book about the individuals within the company, although I worked with many fine people during my years there. No, what I am interested in getting across to the reader are my views on the value of Ikea's example. These views are not based on scientific research, and they're unlikely to stand up to the scrutiny of academic papers; rather, they come from my reflections. Hopefully some of it will strike a chord with you.

CHAPTER 1

The Four Cornerstones of a Good Business

Companies should seek to deliver value in a broader sense than merely returning value to shareholders. They have a larger social mission beyond profit. What are the important prerequisites for retail companies to deliver true value? There are four main points.

1. **A vision with a social ambition combined with a strong value base.** This vision is the very foundation of the business. It defines who you are and how you do things—how you make decisions, what behaviors you exhibit, and what strategies you employ. Building strong values and creating a vision with a social ambition will help you improve not only your profitability but it will also help you gain the respect and trust within society at large.
2. **A business model wherein the product range and price are the main differentiators between you and the competition.** You achieve this business model through company control of the entire value chain from product development and production to retail outlets.
3. **Market leadership and a balanced global portfolio of markets that defines the company's short- and long-term growth**

ambitions. To leverage risk and prepare for future growth, you must establish a healthy mix of mature markets and future growth markets.

4. **Company control by a committed owner.** This will ensure important criteria for success, such as a long-term perspective and a willingness to take risk, as well as establish a company heritage, a purpose, and strong values.

I will discuss these points in the subsequent sections of the book. Although Ikea is the primary business example throughout the book, I do think that the majority of the points I am making apply to the entire retail sector. Some of these concepts—primarily the parts about vision, values, and ownership structure—are even more general and could have some relevance to any business sector. The reader will of course make his or her own judgment about what is of interest.

Detailed Discussions of the Four Cornerstones

You will notice that the four cornerstones are interlinked and dependent on each other. The vision, values, and owner control have a strong influence on the business model and the globalization agenda. They are also important prerequisites for taking the step from being a company that is merely profitable to becoming one that contributes to a better society.

In the first part, I concern myself with explaining the importance of the vision and values in establishing the scope of the business—why vision and values are important; what they could, can, and should be; and how they influence the organization. As well, I will present some thoughts on developing and maintaining a company culture that reflects these values. I take up the often-controversial subject of diversity and why it makes good business sense to build a diverse organization. We'll also take a look at how developing a social and environmental agenda rests on the company's vision and culture as well as on the commitment of managers and employees in carrying it out. Finally, I take the example of one market and show how a company can engage many different stakeholders in an emerging society and make a difference.

In the second part, we turn to the practical questions of "differentiation through control of the value chain," elaborating on what companies actually do and how the day-to-day business is conducted. I will offer my advice on how to develop a strong business model and its ingredients, such as the product range, supply chain, and retail stores. This part also covers how to manage the transformation from a small to a big global company and how to build an organization that effectively supports the entire value chain from product development, production, supply, and sales through its own stores.

The third part deals with the geographical scope of the company. I discuss how companies can decide what markets they should be in and the different challenges and business strategies that may be relevant for global companies.

In the fourth part, you'll learn the merits of different ownership structures to support a successful business and the importance of building for the long term.

Chapter 19, "The Role of the CEO," falls outside the scope of the four cornerstones of a good business and is a more personal reflection. Finally, I will summarize the main points of the book and give my view on the prospects for developing companies in the direction discussed throughout the book.

Ikea as a Model—Good and Bad

My experience at Ikea and the story of this company will be used to illustrate and exemplify my four cornerstones of successful retailing. Thus the reader will also gain insights into the workings of that company. This is not to imply that all of Ikea's decisions have been perfect—like any company it has made mistakes—but I believe it's a good model for the kind of business I wish others would build.

The company Ikea was registered in the small town Älmhult, Sweden, in 1943. The first 67 years of its existence, up until 2010, could be summed up in three distinctive phases.

1. The development of the business model and the values
2. The development of the vision and the retail expansion in Europe
3. The transformation to a big global retailer

During the first phase, covering the 30 years from 1943 to 1972, the company established the business idea, the value base, and the most significant components of the company's concept. In other words, these were the foundations that the company lives by, and upon which the company still rests. Sales reached $58.2 million (€40 million).

The second phase, from 1973 to 1998, was the period where the vision was formulated (1976) and the importance of a strong corporate culture in an international setting was established. In this period, Ikea underwent an expansion that was predominantly European with regard to stores; with regard to sourcing, it was global. Out of 27 retail markets in 2010, 19 were added in this 25-year period. Three had been opened before that period (Sweden, Denmark, and Norway), and five markets were to be opened later. Sales increased to $9.5 billion (€6.5 billion) by 1998.

The third phase of Ikea's development began in 1999 and is ongoing. In this period, Ikea more decisively has begun the transformation from a "small" entrepreneurial company to a structured, efficient global giant (for better or for worse). Sales in the 10 years from 1999 to 2009 tripled from $10 billion (€7 billion) to $31 billion (€21.5 billion).

The Growth of the Ikea Philosophy

During Ikea's growth over these three phases, its management and founder have gradually evolved the philosophy outlined above as the four cornerstones of good business. These guidelines have been key to the company's success and its expansion from a national to a global brand. Had the company not had these cornerstones in place by 1999, it would have been limited in its ability to grow revenues at the pace it did during the following decade.

Ikea's story in the third phase of its expansion is notable precisely because it was during this same period that some businesses that had been viewed as leaders within their industries came to a resounding crash—notably Enron and WorldCom, although there were a number of smaller instances as well.

In the following chapters, I will demonstrate how these four cornerstones were essential to Ikea's success story and how they have broad applicability within the business community throughout the world.

PART 1

A Vision of Social Responsibility

Reading the press and watching television, you can easily get the impression that what counts in the business world is stock value, options, and bonuses to managers. Many suggest that business exists primarily for the purpose of enriching the owners and managers and no one else. If society benefits, it is a side effect—admirable but hardly necessary or innate to good business management.

There is nothing wrong with business creating wealth for owners and managers, but contributing to a better society is important for several reasons:

1. Companies are better equipped than any other institutions to actually help improve people's lives—they have the capacity to reduce poverty, improve the environment, and increase the standard of living for most people.
2. Most people want more from their lives than just to earn their keep, provide for their family, and live for the moment. With a greater purpose than just making money, companies can provide a larger meaning in work and life for their many employees, which is something many people look for.
3. Companies that include a social ambition in their vision statement and live up to it will also improve the likelihood of making profits because they will gain the respect and trust of society as a whole.
4. Organizations that attempt to do good will be more competitive in the labor market so that they can recruit, motivate, and retain the best people.

Ikea is a good example of this. One of the company's biggest strengths is its strong vision—a vision with a social ambition: "To create a better everyday life for the majority of people." This vision was formulated and published in 1976 in a document called "The Testament of a Furniture Dealer."

In his "testament," founder Ingvar Kamprad pointed out that most objects, beautiful and of high quality, are developed only for the rich. He explained that Ikea wanted to change this standard and enable people with limited financial means to have access to home furnishing of high design and good quality.

Kamprad elaborated on the vision statement:

> In all countries and social systems, eastern as well as western, a disproportionately large part of all resources are used to satisfy a small part of the population. In our line of business for instance, too many new and beautiful designed products can be afforded by only a small group of better-off people. Ikea's aim is to change this situation.

Take a moment to consider this concept. It indicates that businesses can take the lead in demonstrating the application of social policy, in creating a structure through which ordinary people can live the kinds of lives they've only dreamed of. Ikea was intended to make the kind of quality products afforded by the rich available to everyone else. This isn't just good social policy; it's good business policy.

I have never seen a better-formulated vision statement anywhere than what Kamprad wrote for Ikea. Why is that?

1. It's incredibly motivating and creates a clear direction for the organization.
2. It provides a vision that is a constant source of inspiration to all Ikea employees.
3. It is important in attracting and keeping good people.

How does the vision of "creating a better everyday life for the majority of people" manifest itself in an organization like Ikea? To what extent does it influence the decision making, strategies, and behavior of the company?

Elements of Good Policy

This is really the question: how does a company put these sorts of policies into practice? Many companies aspire to good social policy, but how many of them are able to express these policies in their day-to-day business expressions?

Let's look at some examples of how these features manifested themselves at Ikea.

Pricing

The most obvious example of Ikea's social vision is reflected in its pricing philosophy. The company's focus is on decreasing sales prices to customers and making products affordable to more and more people. The logic of the financial model to achieve profits but at the same time be affordable is in tune with the vision for the company. Lower sales prices deliver higher sales volume. In combination with keeping costs at a minimum, this policy delivered a bottom-line result. Contrary to many retailers, the company didn't focus on improving the gross margin. Instead, it wanted to develop its top line revenues.

It spared no efforts to find ways to decrease the buying costs of the products. However, unlike many companies, it reinvested these improvements in lower sales prices to the customers, and did not primarily use them in improving the margins. This is a very different business model compared to most other retail companies.

Herein we see one of the basic elements of the Ikea model. The company focused on developing its customer base, even if it meant, in the short run, sacrificing its profit margins. Some companies, where bottom line profit and shareholder wealth are the most important objectives, focus only on improving gross margin. They put their efforts into creating a brand reputation that allows premium prices. Their pricing strategy is limited to monitoring competition and keeping price reductions to a minimum. If they succeed in reducing buying costs, this translates into higher margins and better bottom line profits. The first element of the Ikea success formula is this: *In line with the company vision, the company concentrated on creating savings that could be passed on to its customers.*

Functionality

Vision is also reflected in the company's business decisions concerning functionality in the range of products developed. Solutions that really improve everyday life in people's homes are more important than fancy designs. Design at the expense of functionality will, in the long run, lead to losing customers. That is why Ikea is focused intently on creating solutions for storage and for people living in small spaces. The company recognized that most people don't live in mansions; they need to find reasonable spaces to put their possessions, where those objects will be readily available, and they need to make the most efficient use of the space they have.

Customer Involvement

This importance of vision is also demonstrated by the Ikea mantra that people have more time than money. In other words, the company rewards its customers for their involvement in the distribution of the company's products. The more your customers do, the less they pay. The entire sales system is based on integrating the customer in the distribution process. The customers not only choose, pick, and pay for the products they want, they transport and assemble these products themselves. By using this system, Ikea can keeps its costs low and thus reduce its prices even more. This principle is often put to the test. But so far the idea has prevailed: if you want more service from Ikea, you have to pay more. Correspondingly, if you're willing to do more, you'll ultimately pay a lower price. Customers who choose to do everything themselves should always have the best deal. This way there is an option for those with limited financial means.

Expansion

That vision should be aligned with the company's business practices is also exemplified in Ikea's expansion strategy. Soon after the collapse of the Soviet Union at the end of the 1980s, Ikea began retail operations in the former Eastern European countries, and in Russia in 1999. Although many companies have contemplated business opportunities in emerging markets, Ikea's social vision to assist those less well off played an important role in pushing the firm's sometimes high-risk projects into early realization.

Environmentalism

During the past few years, the importance of a company developing an environmental and social agenda has risen. Many companies have struggled and are still struggling internally to gain acceptance for such programs. On occasion, these sorts of discussions have roiled Ikea's organization. Perhaps the very strong commitment from managers and employees has enabled the company to take the lead when setting a challenging environmental agenda. The company's vision, promoted from the top down, has been instrumental in gaining this acceptance at all levels of the organization.

Improving environmental and social conditions is totally aligned with the vision of creating a better everyday life for the many. Ingvar Kamprad has said that Ikea has a duty to grow. He meant by this that Ikea must not confine itself to becoming the biggest or best, or to make the shareholders and managers wealthier. No, a duty to grow means a duty to realize the vision of creating a better everyday life for the majority of people in society.

Gaining Credibility for Its Vision

Many companies try to formulate a vision with a social ambition. The challenge in today's cynical world is to make this vision credible. Ikea is credible—the fact that it is not a public company helps. Ikea does not have to balance the potential conflict between maximizing shareholder wealth and achieving its social vision.

More important, Ikea is credible because it delivers on what it says—with the products, the home furnishing solutions, the low prices, and the conduct of its employees.

People believe the company's leaders when they say they're committed to improving society and the environment. Today there is a genuine conviction at all levels in the company that Ikea's social and environmental work is an important part of defining it as a company—not only what it says but what it *does*.

A social vision is meaningless unless it is realized and reflected every day in your company's actions. If a company wants to build a deep and long lasting relationship with its customers, employees, suppliers, and other stakeholders, what will matter is not just what you do; of equal or perhaps even greater importance is who you are and how you do it. In Ikea's case, it took 30 years before the vision was formulated. Ideally, of course, both vision and values should be developed early on in the development of a company.

If vision and values are created with genuine intentions, they will have a fundamental influence on the direction, strategies, decisions, and behavior of the company. Most important, they will serve as a tremendous motivational force that can attract, keep, and inspire all employees to contribute to the best of their potential. They will create a bond with customers and contribute to gaining the respect of society at large. I cannot overstress the importance of this point for the success and reputation of an organization.

In the following chapters, I will discuss in more detail some examples of stakeholder engagements that can contribute to the broader objective of contributing to a better society.

CHAPTER 2

Maintaining a Strong and Dynamic Corporate Culture

The challenge of attracting and retaining good people is something all retail companies struggle with, bringing to the forefront issues including:

- High turnover of staff
- The best managers being headhunted by competitors
- A general reluctance to work in retail because of working hours, workload, low pay, etc.

To determine the best way to meet these challenges, we need to unravel some of the concerns by managers and workers that lead to it. What factors are important to managers and employees when looking for a job or staying with their employer? Is the way to attract and retain good people simply to pay the highest salary? From some of the discussions that go on concerning bonuses and stock options, you can easily get the impression that what counts is who earns the most.

Setting high salaries as a strategy is a dangerous path to follow. Although you may initially find that your prospective pool of employees is broadened, you risk attracting people who are primarily motivated by money. They have no real allegiance to the company, and they are likely to leave you as soon as someone comes along who pays a bit more.

In fact, many surveys show that more than money, employees value job security, recognition, a sense of belonging, professional development possibilities, and working conditions. Salary usually comes further down the list as long as it is reasonable and fair.

Ikea's policy regarding the salaries the company pays is to position itself in the middle of the market. The salaries Ikea offers its employees must be fair, but they must not be the main reason for choosing to work for the company.

Many companies supplement salary with a complex network of bonuses, stock incentive programs, stock options, and other features. I confess that in most cases I prefer working with a straight salary. I do believe in ownership involvement in the business. Offering managers the possibility to acquire shares in the company is great; however, when these are acquired through a stock incentive program as an additional form of compensation, they often seem to miss the point. Too often they are overgenerous and short-term. With very limited investment of their own money in shares, managers carry very little risk, in combination with a fairly short-term program time (often three years). Such a situation risks diluting the whole point of ownership—commitment and long-term thinking and actions.

The Value of Bonuses

Bonuses can be appropriate when you need to focus individuals or the organization on a very specific task. If bonuses are used, in my opinion they should normally not exceed a maximum of three to four months of salary per year. Another possibility is to institute a very broad bonus program through which, ideally, all employees can participate in the success of the company. Workers are motivated by a moderate compensation that recognizes that when the company does well, I as an employee can share in that success.

Overly generous salaries, bonuses, and option programs for top managers have too many downsides. They risk alienating managers from the workers, who feel their salaries are under constant pressure while managers receive excessive compensation. For instance, in the United States in 2010, median CEO salaries increased 27 percent, while worker pay increased 2.1 percent. It can also create a culture of greed and suggests that money is what keeps managers loyal to the company.

There is plenty of evidence to suggest that extensive bonus programs lead to very short-term thinking and actions. We have seen the consequences of this in the finance sector but also in many other companies. Excessive compensation usually results in a negative perception of the company among customers, the media, authorities, and other stakeholders. It is not always easy for a company to opt out of this system, particularly when everybody else is doing it. Some sort of legislation could be one solution to level the playing field; however, even without legislation, it can be done. I think this has been proven in many private companies. With a strong owner present, compensation tends to remain at a more moderate level without the company losing good people. In 1984, Peter Drucker suggested that an executive's salary should be no more than 20 times that of an average employee. Today, total executive compensation—including salaries, bonuses, etc.—can often be 50 times or more than an average employee's compensation.

Big, renowned companies have some advantages when attracting competent people.

- Being a well-recognized brand is an advantage.
- Being international implies many career opportunities.
- Being perceived as relatively successful implies job security and personal success for the individual working for the company.

Most companies work hard to provide training and development opportunities, improving leadership skills among their managers and improving working conditions and benefits as a means to retain and motivate their people. These are the things that all retailers do, although some have proven better at it than others.

To attract and retain the best people, a company needs a strong competitive advantage in the labor market—something that is difficult to copy. *I believe a strong company culture is just such an advantage.*

The Structure of a Company Culture

What is a company culture? An informal definition might be that it is simply "the way we do things around here." Ask someone about the company culture at their organization, and chances are you'll get an explanation of the attitude and approach to the daily work that's common throughout the company. A number of more or less informal rules and values give guidance on how daily work should be approached, and these form the nucleus of the company culture—but they are not all of it. These rules and values should be strongly connected to the vision and business idea. Therefore, you can say that the company culture's foremost aim is to assist in the realization of the corporate vision and business idea.

Companies that develop and cultivate their own identity—their own company culture—by creating their own values, standards, and informal rules have an advantage over others. Such a culture has three important attributes:

1. **Creating belonging and fellowship.** This in turn radiates security and strength, and they give the organization efficiency and success.
2. **Bringing employees together.** Containing clear moral and ethical principals, it gives guidance to their behavior, persuading them to do what is right in all situations and accept the consequences. This will be a stronger guardian against corruption, fraud, and other misbehavior than any policy, guideline, or legal requirement. And, most important, strong moral and ethical values will support a vision with a social ambition and guide corporate actions and behavior toward the broader purpose of contributing to society.

3. Inspiring allegiance to the company. To be employed in a successful company whose culture one appreciates means that one considers work as being more than a meal ticket. Instead, work has something to do with the quality of life.

Strong values certainly give a company a competitive edge in the labor market, both in attracting and retaining good people. Strong values can also be valuable in creating loyalty and credibility among customers and other stakeholders.

Ikea's Company Culture

Now let us look at some examples of Ikea's culture. What are the values and ethics that are embedded in this culture? And how do they influence the company's ability to attract and retain good people?

Simplicity in behavior. One element of a corporate culture is how people working for the company behave toward one another. Do people respect each other regardless of title? This element, if it's properly done, breaks down visible and invisible barriers between manager and employees. At Ikea, people greet each other with first names. Managers and employees on all levels conduct business travel in the same way—there's none of the division between first-class and coach that one sees at many organizations. Managers and employees eat together in the staff canteen. Everyone adopts the same informal and common dress code.

The company tries to eliminate all status symbols and create a trustful relationship between employees and managers. This makes a difference to many workers and entices them to stay with Ikea even when other firms offer them more money.

Delegating and accepting responsibility. Ikea makes a point of giving people a lot of responsibility early on in their careers. This was a very important experience for me personally that created a strong bond to the company. This cultural element also creates a climate in which the managers and their teams share a strong sense of ownership of their stores, where they feel they can influence and develop their business. Many of the store managers get frequent offers from competing companies, often at much higher salary levels, but Ikea rarely lose any of them. Many of them cite the sense of freedom and ownership of their stores as the single biggest reason why they choose to stay.

Daring to be different. Ikea prides itself on its willingness to try other solutions than the established ones. Although much of the daily work for many of the workers is about routines and execution as it is in any company Ikea also encourages everyone to come up with new and better approaches, giving all employees the opportunity to be part of development and change. Daring to be different guided some of the most important development in the business model in the early days of the company.

Striving to meet reality. Understanding the details of all levels of the business is an important part of Ikea's values. Managers must have experience on the shop floor and spend time in the stores and at the suppliers. Ikea promotes this through so called anti-bureaucratic weeks, during which corporate managers are encouraged to take time out from their regular work and spend time working in the stores in order to better understand the realities of the customers and employees. The importance of being grounded in the business, I believe, is one reason why Ikea has had difficulties in recruiting higher management externally. You are simply not accepted by the organization unless you are an authority on every detail of the business, something you can best gain inside the company. You should be a specialist before you become a generalist (manager). You are a better manager if you have a solid competence in one or more areas of importance to the business.

Cost consciousness. No description of the Ikea values would be complete without mentioning the focus on costs. Low costs of course are necessary when your business model is based on low prices. This is a good example of how the corporate values support both the vision and the business idea. Ikea puts much effort into establishing cost consciousness among all its employees in their everyday actions and behavior.

All workers should be engaged in this effort. This is not only important to save costs internally. If a company is to be credible in its discussions with suppliers on the importance of reducing purchase prices, it has to live what it preaches. To be credible to the customers whose life the company wants to improve, the company must show by action that it is putting all its efforts behind this. And to be credible in its environmental efforts, the company must show that it works toward using as few resources as possible. As we can see, cost consciousness has broader implications than just reducing operational costs.

Swedish Values?

Sometimes I am asked if these are typical Swedish values or a typical Swedish management style. The Ikea values are, in my opinion, first and foremost the values of its founder, Ingvar Kamprad. Kamprad was, of course, brought up in and influenced by Swedish society and was steeped in its traditions. In that sense, his values are most likely a reflection of Swedishness in some ways.

Some aspects of Ikea values are fairly common in Sweden. For instance, in Sweden we promote a humble attitude—never talk or brag about your success; always focus on what doesn't work rather than celebrating success. This is a very Swedish trait.

We encourage simplicity, trying to eliminate status symbols and treating everyone equally regardless of titles. This way of thinking sits well with many Swedes who were brought up in a time when Sweden was largely run by a social-democratic government and equality was at the forefront of Swedish politics.

We delegate and accept responsibility. To question authority, be it parents or teachers, is something that is encouraged from childhood in Sweden. To think for yourself and take initiative is part of our upbringing. So giving and accepting responsibility comes easy to many Swedes.

Another aspect of Ikea's culture that might be attributable to its birthplace is the focus on cost consciousness. The area of Sweden (Småland) where Kamprad was raised is well known for its frugal, humble, and hardworking people.

Why do a company's values become what they are? In most cases, they are probably a combination of the needs of the business and the core values of the founder and the social environment in which he was brought up.

The Centrality of Continuity During Expansion

The values are a strong foundation and take a long time to truly anchor in a big organization. Therefore, continuity is important so that the values are not lost or arbitrarily replaced in the transition from one leadership team to the next. However, this need must not prevent companies from being able to reevaluate the components of the company culture from time to time, to make sure they are still relevant to support the business and that they are useful for the new generation of workers.

Examples of "new" company values that are relevant to companies with the ambition to be good corporate citizens are those related to social and environmental commitment and equality through diversity. Concern regarding these matters has risen dramatically over the last few years among customers, managers, and workers. If a company wants to be an attractive employer today and in the future, it must show in its attitude, values, and actions that it has a genuine interest in contributing in these areas.

Let me stress again that company values must retain continuity over time while continuously developing in order to stay relevant to current and future business and social conditions.

Let us again look at the example of Ikea. On the face of it, the company is successful at attracting and retaining good people. During the past five years, the company has been ranked as the most attractive employer among both students and managers in its home market, Sweden. In many other countries, Ikea is ranked among the top 15. New store openings can attract up to 10,000 applications for jobs with little or no recruitment efforts. The turnover of staff, of course, can vary a lot depending on the market, but for managers it is often below 5 percent, and for nonmanagement workers it can vary from 4 percent to 80 percent. In internal surveys, 75 percent of workers say they would strongly recommend Ikea as an employer, and 70 percent feel satisfied with their job most of the time. I suspect that the Ikea company culture provides a very important reason for these good figures.

Let me give an example of how the Ikea values have influenced the development of the company. In 1973, after 30 years of existence, Ikea had seven stores and sales revenues of around $57.4M (€40 million). You may think that this still leaves plenty of room for continued expansion in Sweden and maybe Norway and Denmark. At that point, Sweden had five stores, while Norway and Denmark had only a single store each, but during the next 25 years (1973–1998), the company undertook an aggressive expansion across Europe. The Ikea history documentation tells the story about how the decision was made to try out the concept in Switzerland as a first step. They argued, as the story goes, that Switzerland was the most difficult market in Europe. The thinking was that if Ikea was successful in Switzerland, the company could make it in all other markets. I don't know how well researched this evaluation was and precisely how committed Ikea was to that test.

In fact, looking at it today, I don't think Switzerland was the most difficult market. I might even argue the opposite point of view. The competition was represented by one very traditional high-priced furniture company called Pfister. This left an opening for modern Scandinavian furniture, offering good value at a low price. Ikea would stand out very strongly from the start. To this day, Switzerland has always been one of the European markets with the highest gross margin, also an indicator of the competitive climate.

A Period of Rapid Growth

The move into Switzerland started a phase of rapid expansion into Europe and Canada. In the next 10 years, between 1973 and 1983, Ikea expanded from 7 stores to 41 stores and grew from sales of $57.4M (€40 million) to $861.4M (€600 million), a remarkable growth by any standard. Most of this expansion came from the German market. In 1973, Sweden accounted for 80 percent of Ikea's sales. Ten years later (1983), this was down to

22 percent. Meanwhile, Germany developed from nothing to a share of 45 percent, or almost half of Ikea's sales. Germany has never left that position as the number one Ikea country.

This was a very significant phase for Ikea—not only because of the growth itself but more important because this expansion defined the company. The Ikea culture, embodying its values, was tested during this expansion in a new international environment. The importance of a strong value base in a fast growing international company was an important learning experience. During this period, many of Ikea's most influential managers proved themselves at an early age. Many of these are people who have been crucial to the company up to this day. A cornerstone of the company's practices became the culture of promoting people on potential rather than experience.

This expansion was also the period when Ikea developed a confidence in its ability to grow globally. Not least, they discovered that all markets possessed the same basic needs and values. This realization helped shape the company's thinking around the range development and supply chain.

During this period, the European expansion and the Swedish market (the "mature" home market) were led by two very important—and very different—individuals. Hans Ax, who had opened the first big Stockholm store in 1965, led the mature markets in Scandinavia. Meanwhile, Jan Aulin, who had been the assistant to Ingvar Kamprad, was responsible for the expansion in Europe. Their management styles were different but perfectly suited for their respective challenges. Sweden became the parent who through well-considered careful analysis and strategy developed the Swedish market through new store concepts, marketing strategies, and considerable investments into training and development. In Europe and primarily Germany, on the other hand, all focus was on opening new stores. They copied the Swedish concept, and speed was the priority. Their documentation backing up investment decisions for new stores was limited to a torn-out map from the yellow pages. Sometimes the sites were probably already acquired by the time the proposals reached the board for decision. Management maintained a strong self confidence and "can-do" attitude.

Expanding into Germany

The expansion into Germany is a very good example of the small outsider taking on the giants. In this very big market, because of its strategies and its aggressive stance, Ikea immediately gained a very high level of recognition and success. Part of this can, of course, be explained by the fact that the company maintained a very different business model from traditional German firms. (This will be discussed in the following chapter.) Two other things contributed strongly. One was the very powerful and different marketing Ikea used ("daring to be different"); the other was the Ikea company culture.

Germany, growing out of its national culture, had a formal and controlled business environment. This left Germans to be charmed by the Swedish retailer's total lack of "formal behavior." Managers wore jeans and T-shirts and expressed a desire to be addressed by their employees as if they were close friends ("simplicity in the behavior"). There were no frills, no perks, and Ikea's managers displayed an incredible confidence in their ideas and concepts. Customers loved the range, the prices, the "crazy" marketing and store events, the staff attitude, and the challenging behavior. However, with the speed of expansion and lack of systems and structure, the quality and availability of the products was inadequate. In these first years of Ikea's German presence, a love-hate relationship with customers developed. Nonetheless, to this day, these first defining years are still fondly remembered by many German customers. I still think of Germany as Ikea's second home market. Together with Sweden, it is the backbone of the company.

In 1983, when I started at Ikea, I was 26 years old. I was just out of college with a BA in business and an MA in economics. After an introductory period and one year working in Switzerland, I moved to Germany and became the business controller of the retail operations and a member of the German management team. I suspect that promoting me to that role with my limited experience was probably a braver decision than giving me the CEO job in 1999. I was certainly more nervous! This was a perfect example of the company's philosophy of promoting young people based on potential rather than experience. This gave me and many others with similar experience a unique opportunity to take on responsibility in our early years ("delegating and accepting responsibility").

The German experience of Ikea—and my parallel career within the company—was a classic example of how corporate values can contribute to the success of a company. When you get it right, it can have enormous leverage. My three years in Germany were among the most important periods of my life in Ikea. The learning curve was very steep, and my affection and loyalty to the company was forged. After that early experience, I couldn't imagine working for another company. The reason for this loyalty was the shared value system—the informal attitude, the possibility to influence and take responsibility, the cost consciousness, the confidence, the human touch, the good friends. I felt at home.

Finding the Right People

Finding people who thrive in this type of environment is relatively easy in most countries. However, one must also recognize that in some markets, upbringing, religion, norms, and values are very different from the Western way of thinking. And we must also recognize that increasingly we'll be coming into contact with these markets.

By way of illustration, let me share a couple of reflections on the meeting between the Chinese culture and the Ikea culture. Ikea has had a strong presence in China both in terms of supply and retail. If I can generalize, based on a number of years of intimate contact with Chinese officials and local Chinese Ikea employees, I would say that in China it is not acceptable to make mistakes. You do not argue with managers. Knowledge is regarded as power, and managers hold on to it, instead of sharing and developing others' talents. The focus is the individual, not the team. Further, in China, a certain distance is maintained between managers and employees. These are all values that are in conflict with the Ikea way of doing business.

On the other hand, in China you also find a high level of curiosity and enthusiasm. There is a strong entrepreneurial spirit. Everyone works hard. There is a willingness to learn and develop. It does take a long time to build trust, but when you gain it, it is very strong. These are values that fit very well with those upheld by Ikea.

In markets such as China, one needs to consider long and carefully before introducing and establishing Western company values, like those of Ikea. It is important to recognize the differences between local cultures and the values of your own company. You need to understand the Chinese way, and you need to support the Chinese managers so that they can also succeed in a "Western" company environment. You need to be crystal clear on what your company's values are. You must have more patience than usual, because it will take time for the Chinese managers to fully absorb these values, which are substantially different from those they have grown up with. You must coach and mentor the Chinese managers more than usual, because if you are to succeed in China, you must be able to promote Chinese managers to senior positions both in China and in other markets.

Thinking Globally

In 2010, Ikea employed around 125,000 people in 44 countries. The company was increasingly faced with the problem of maintaining and reinforcing a company culture in a fast-expanding organization operating amid many different national cultures.

The first key to success in this endeavor is to see the company culture as a fundamental foundation for your business. It is as important as the vision, business idea, and core concepts.

The company culture is the glue that keeps the organization together, that makes the company different from all others. It is, quite simply, the soul of the company. To keep it strong, therefore, it has to be integral to everything you do.

Ikea started this at the level of recruitment. In the recruitment process, the company used "value based recruitment" in all parts of the company. This helps the recruiters determine if candidates are suitable for Ikea not only from a standpoint of technical competence in the positions for which they're applying, but also whether they share the company's values.

The company continued its value-centric approach in all management review processes. When a manager is considered for promotion, the company asks if her or his performance and leadership reflects the company's values. Ikea establishes this in different ways, but one of the most important is an evaluation format in which workers anonymously give their feedback on their manager. This practice is maintained at all levels of the company, from the shop floor to the corporate boardroom. In 2008, 70 percent of workers participating in this survey said that their manager acted as a good role model for the Ikea values. As well as identifying candidates for promotion, this tool helps identify, give feedback to, and improve the leadership skills of those with low scores.

The Ikea culture is also an integral part of many training programs throughout the company, not least the induction and leadership training courses.

But at the end of the day, the most important point is that the leaders of the company must be living examples of the values; Ikea's culture must be reflected in everything they do. This is something they can never delegate away or compromise on. *Managers with bad results and good values should be given a second chance. Managers with good results and bad values should be asked to leave.* Only when you are not willing to compromise on this do you show the organization by your actions the importance you give the company culture.

Building Over Time

Building a strong company culture takes time and consistency. It may take as many as 10 or 20 years to integrate it into the DNA of the company. This is a reason for the central importance of continuity in ownership and management. In the case of Ikea, the founder is still there after 65 years, and during those decades the company has had only three CEOs, all internal promotions. Company owners with a shorter time perspective have a competitive disadvantage in the areas of vision and values, points that go to the heart of building credibility and motivation among different stakeholders.

There is no doubt in my mind that companies that build a strong company culture that is adapted to their business have a powerful marketplace advantage. The company culture not only contributes internally to the strength of the company by clarifying what behavior is expected from workers and management, it also helps you in making the right decisions and creates motivation. Further, it enables you to build brand identity externally with your customers and other stakeholders, which in turn provides a powerful advantage in attracting and retaining good people. In the labor market, you're not focused on selling products; rather, you're competing to attract the skills and knowledge of other people. Your strength in attracting good people lies in work with meaning (the vision), good working relationships, recognition, respect, and development opportunities (common values).

CHAPTER 3

Diversity: A Good Business Choice

As the new CEO of Ikea in 1999, I began to assemble a new management team. Among my first actions, I promoted two women into senior positions. One, as the manager of Ikea of Sweden AB (Ltd.), was responsible for the product range and supply chain; the other became manager of our retail operations in North America. These promotions prompted very strong reactions from inside the company. Up to that point, senior management in Ikea had been entirely composed of middle-aged Swedish white men. The "glass ceiling" was very strong, without a crack in it. Making these appointments shattered that ceiling, and a wave of emotions tumbled out. It quickly became clear that many competent people within the company didn't feel recognized for the job they were doing and felt that a "boys club" was running the company.

Reasons to Be a Diverse Company

Diversity in business was and still is a hot topic. According to many, progress on this front is too slow. Others argue that businesses are moving too quickly and that a concern for diversity is being exercised at the expense of good business decisions. Is the drive for a diverse management team a question of fairness, a good business strategy, or a bit of both? I think probably the latter. Strictly from a business perspective, there are at least four good reasons to promote diversity.

1. **Customer focus.** If a company wants to understand its customers and, for that matter, its employees, I believe it is important that management teams reflect the diversity among these groups. Seventy percent of Ikea customers are women, and ethnic minorities account for a significant number of customers in many store catchment areas. The company will understand these business opportunities better if these groups are represented within the management.
2. **Decision making.** When everybody thinks the same, not much creative thinking happens. Any management team will thrive from being challenged and looking at issues from different perspectives. Conversely, if a company promotes only people from a similar background, meetings may be more comfortable, but they'll probably be a lot less productive.
3. **Recruitment.** I haven't seen any scientific evidence that middle-aged Swedish white men are better at home furnishing retailing than others. On the other hand, companies are missing out on attracting the best competence if they don't show in their actions that everyone has equal opportunities based on ability. An ambitious person looking for the right company to join will make decisions based in part on whether she thinks she will be welcome in that organization. A diverse management team says, in effect, that everyone is welcome based on their talents and ideas, not on their gender or skin color.
4. **Motivation.** Recognition is a very strong motivational force. When you promote someone or even hold out the prospect of promotion, you create a lot of motivation. Thus, it's extremely important for employees to know that the company philosophy on promotion is based on meritocracy.

However, even with these evident business reasons, change regarding diversity is slow. If it is to speed up, some barriers must be demolished. The biggest hurdle to overcome is most likely prejudice. Not many people would admit that they have prejudices against women or ethnic minorities, to mention just two examples. But in reality, this is the main barrier to change. To overcome this, we need to address these prejudices, and once we accept that they exist, we must be willing to change. The biggest reason for the slow pace of change in many companies is that management underestimates or does not want to address this issue.

A Campaign for Diversity

What did we do at Ikea? The promotion of two women to very senior positions in 1999 sent a strong message. We followed this up with leadership seminars in which managers from all parts of Ikea met together in an effort to promote the idea that we were all part of one company with a single set of values. These seminars also addressed some of the issues concerning diversity. We expanded the management review process to monitor progress on diversity in different parts of the organization. We set as a goal that the management teams should ideally reflect the diversity of the Ikea customers and workers.

After 10 years, we've seen much progress in the promotion of women within the retail part of the business. In 2008, Ikea had 35 percent women store managers, up from 15 percent in the mid nineties. Women country managers were 30 percent and deputy country managers 50 percent in 2008. In 1999, the ratio of Swedes to non-Swedes in management teams outside Sweden was approximately one in three. By the end of the first decade of the twenty-first century, this had fallen to one in six—a considerable change. Promoting ethnic minorities, on the other hand, has shown very little progress.

The work on diversity has helped improve the quality and motivation of the Ikea management teams. However, change in this area needs constant attention from management; otherwise it will not happen. Personally, I am not in favor of the suggestion that female representation on company boards should be subject to legislation, as is being done in Norway and Sweden. The managers of companies have far greater opportunities to influence diversity than their boards. This is where the focus must be, but not through legislation. It is a more significant step to change the diversity ratio within management than within the board.

Making strong business arguments for diversity, citing better management and decision making, is the best way to promote such diversity and holds the greatest likelihood of success. But there is a moral issue here too. Who wants to work in a company that is not considered fair and does not give all people equal opportunities to succeed based on ability?

Finally, taking action to be diverse makes you a better corporate citizen. Poverty is a big social problem in Western countries, not least among ethnic minorities. The best way to address the problem is to create job opportunities for these groups. Only the business community can accomplish this. Governments can provide social welfare and education, but that is only part of the solution. Jobs—by which I mean good jobs, not just the ones at the bottom of the pay scale—are the best way to alleviate poverty.

CHAPTER 4

The Environmental Agenda

s an environmental vision and activity bad for business?

How you answer this question will determine the level of commitment your company gives to environmental issues. If you view such work primarily as a cost to the business, your commitment will most likely be minimal. The company will follow the law regarding environmental regulations—at best it will conduct a few PR activities, and if a crisis occurs, it will take the necessary corrective actions.

To take a more proactive, forceful, and credible approach, companies need to see environmental work as something more than reaction to problems. Better still, they need to flee the mentality that views it as essentially a public relations issue. They must understand that not only is maintaining environmental standards a cost (and, as such, a potential threat to profitability and shareholder value), but in fact environmental work can contribute to *increased* profitability, more motivated workers, and a long-term strengthened position in a market. A strong environmental stand, in other words, represents a potential market advantage. Customers and other stakeholders can genuinely feel that the company values have aligned with their own and that the company actively contributes to a better society.

Accepting Environmentalism as a Value

How can you reach a broad acceptance of a social and environmental agenda in an organization?

First, it is important that the CEO takes a clear stand. The majority of employees are unlikely to have a defined opinion one way or the other. This is a complex question with many different views among influential opinion leaders. It requires a good deal of knowledge to feel confident about it. Therefore, many employees need clear guidance from the management before they feel comfortable about the chosen direction.

Another important point is to make sure that managers who are promoted share the values of the top management on this issue. Environmental issues today are more emotional than many others, questions that will touch the core values of the individuals. Managers will be on the front line of any efforts your company makes in this area, and they must believe in what they're doing. Remember: no commitment, no action.

It's a good sign when you start to get clear support from employees, customers, media, and NGOs. This helps to convince those who are still doubtful.

A further help in this regard is to prove that fears of increased costs are unfounded. For Ikea, this was relatively easy—in most cases, what is good for the environment means using fewer resources; using fewer resources most often results in lower costs, which Ikea has been able to pass along to our customers.

Environmental activism can mean your company will have the opportunity to create useful alliances with different NGOs, such as Greenpeace, World Wildlife Federation, Save the Children, and UNICEF. These organizations are valuable for advice; they can also help you widen the base of your support and achieve results.

Your company's vision, business idea, and values must align with and support environmental work. The Ikea vision "to create a better everyday life for many people" fits perfectly with this notion. Its business idea, "to offer a range at prices so low that the majority can afford them," also aligns very well. As I said, low prices require low costs, and low costs means using less resources.

Finally, as with all successful business work, you need clear goals, strategies, plans, resources, and division of responsibility. These must be well known and anchored throughout the organization.

The Ikea Environmental Record

Today, I can look back at Ikea during my tenure and feel confident that the company has a strong and well-anchored record of proactive environmental work. This work has been good for the business, but reaching this point was not always a smooth ride.

In the eighties and nineties, Ikea received some serious criticism from the media regarding its environmental practices. In both cases, the company's leadership were neither well prepared to respond, nor were they fully aware of the problem.

The first such incident occurred in the eighties when tests revealed that the board-based furniture products contained unacceptably high levels of formaldehyde, something that had not been properly controlled. The second incident, in the nineties, concerned accusations of child labor in the supplier's factories in Pakistan. Although never verified, this was a situation that also was not properly controlled.

Thus, the situation for Ikea in 1999 included some bad experience in the recent past. We also lacked a clear strategy on how to move forward. The company faced its problems defensively and reactively. This was a big concern to me; I felt strongly that Ikea, with its vision "to be for the majority of people," needed to be at the forefront on these issues. I was also convinced that a strong environmental stand made good business sense. Although the interest among the general public was not at the level it is today (global warming had not yet entered widespread public awareness), environmental issues were a growing concern in society, and Ikea needed to take a stance. Social and environmental work became an important priority in the "Ten Jobs in Ten Years" long-term direction (10/10)—a plan I'll discuss shortly.

Initially, I faced a lot of skepticism within the company, which stimulated many animated discussions in management and within the board. The concern raised was not *if* Ikea should do something, but *how much* should be done and *how quickly* the company should move forward.

These were the questions that caused most internal debate:

- Will greater environmental work increase costs and therefore injure profitability, competitiveness, and long-term survival for the company?
- Are these issues Ikea's responsibility or the responsibility of governments and suppliers?
- How serious is the environmental threat to our society?
- Should the company let others steer the agenda for environmental activism, or should we steer it ourselves?

Reflecting on these discussions today, I am happy that we took the time to really discuss these issues internally. As I've said earlier, it is only when you accept a value with your heart that there will be real commitment in its implementation.

The Evolution of Ikea's Strategies

Back in 1999 at Ikea, the company's priorities were a bit different from those it held by 2009. In 1999, the company leadership was focused on three issues:

- The conditions at the suppliers
- Forestry
- The content of the products

These were, of course, all important areas, given the business Ikea was operating, but the company was also increasingly influenced by criticism from the media and NGOs regarding its environmental policies, which in turn affected each of these three areas. Supplier relations were important, since an increasing share of products were sourced from emerging markets with often poor working conditions and a poor environmental record in the factories. The issue of child labor in Pakistan being used to create company products brought this matter to a head; no one in the company wanted to end up in a situation like that again.

Forestry was a priority for Ikea, since wood is a core material for the company's products. Forestry was also an important focus area for NGOs such as Greenpeace and WWF.

Finally, many customers were increasingly concerned with purchasing healthy products, ones that contained no toxic substances and created no environmental hazards in their production. Energy consumption and climate change were part of the company's plan, but the awareness was not yet at the level it is today. Therefore, the company leadership confined its efforts to transportation issues.

Putting Codes in Place

Between 2000 and 2009, the company spent time and money improving the conditions at Ikea's suppliers. In 2000, we established the Ikea code of conduct (IWAY). The code specifies the minimum requirements placed on suppliers, including compliance with national legislation, no forced or child labor, no discrimination, payment of at least the minimum wage and compensation for overtime, a safe and healthy working environment, and responsibility for waste, emissions, and the handling of chemicals. The checklist of around ninety questions is used by Ikea's approximately 80 auditors at the company's 1,200 suppliers worldwide (2009). When there is noncompliance, the auditors help set up action plans, find solutions, and conduct follow-up visits to review progress. In 2009, more than 100,000 deviations had been registered, of which the majority were corrected. This figure is a good indication that this policy is improving standards at the suppliers.

On a global level, Ikea has a compliance and monitoring group, responsible for calibrating evaluation standards and ensuring that the same audit criteria are followed worldwide. On top of that, third-party auditors such as KPMG and PricewaterhouseCoopers participate in order to verify Ikea working methods and audit results. This last is important to establish credibility externally. More than 1,000 audits (internal and external) are completed each year.

The average IWAY fulfillment for all of Ikea was 93 percent in 2009, but there have been some areas of concern that have proven very difficult to deal with. Most challenging are the working conditions at Ikea suppliers in China. China, together with Poland, is Ikea's most important sourcing market, supplying more than 20 percent of all the company's sourcing. Correct information is often difficult to get from the suppliers. Legislation is often not implemented properly, and the Chinese government often inadequately enforces it. Interestingly, China, as a communist country, has very liberal labor legislation regarding working hours, overtime compensation, and other related issues, on par with countries such as Sweden.

I can understand the dilemma this situation poses for Chinese authorities, as they obviously do not want to lose the competitiveness of their export industry. Ikea has tried various ways of improving the situation over the years, with limited success. One alternative is to increase the penalties for noncompliance, but the best way probably is to increase the company share of each supplier's total output. By adopting this policy, compliance becomes more important for the suppliers. Unfortunately, it is a slow process to increase the motivation in the supplier base to improve working and environmental conditions.

One of the most important concerns of IWAY is to prevent the use of child labor by suppliers and their subcontractors. This has been a focus for many years, especially in India. Ikea cooperates with UNICEF and Save the Children to tackle the root cause of child labor and to achieve sustainable solutions.

Lasting change requires a holistic approach that involves understanding the children's situation and undertaking long-term programs to address the root causes such as poverty, ill health, and ignorance. Together with UNICEF, the company has been involved in this work since 2000. The project focuses on creating awareness and mobilizing the rural communities around actions to prevent child labor. These include establishing women self-help groups, giving women basic education, providing bridge schools for children who have not attended schools, and offering immunization for children and mothers against common illnesses.

Forestry

Forestry has been another important part of the company's environmental strategy, since most of Ikea's products are built from wood. The long-term goal of the program is to source all wood used in Ikea products from forests certified as responsibly managed. It's proven more difficult than anyone thought to increase the amount of certified wood used in the company's products. Ikea has worked for many years with WWF to improve forest management and combat illegal logging in key wood-sourcing countries such as Russia, China, Romania, and Vietnam. The result of this long and arduous struggle is that by 2009, 94 percent of suppliers met the basic Ikea forestry requirements. However, only a very limited number were certified as responsibly managed—so this program has a long way to go.

Raw Materials

When Ikea reviewed its environmental strategy in 2009, it shifted the focus somewhat. The company turned to greater efforts in the areas of efficient use of raw materials (including but not confined to wood) and climate change.

Ikea products are designed to maximize the use of the raw material (hence minimizing waste) and to optimize the means of production. For example, where possible the company tries to optimize the production chain, meaning sawmills are built close to the forests where the logs are cut, and furniture production facilities are then positioned close to the sawmills. If it can, Ikea tries to locate different furniture production units in one area, facilities that can use different parts of the log. Thereby, use of the raw material can be maximized, and the transportation during the production process can be minimized. This concept is used by the Ikea Industry Group, Swedwood.

Ikea is continuously developing new production techniques and designs to decrease the use of raw materials. One example is the board on frame technique, of which Ikea is the leading developer. In this technique, a core of stiff paperlike card is sandwiched between thin sheets of wood. This and similar techniques will eventually be used in most if not all Ikea furniture products. I would not be surprised if solid wood is phased out of production altogether and replaced by furniture "look alike" techniques like board on frame.

Climate Change

Although CO_2 reduction has always been on Ikea's sustainability agenda, I think it is fair to say that it has grown significantly in importance over the past few years.

The Ikea carbon footprint can be defined in many different ways. If everything is included—that is, the extraction of raw material at source, the processing at subsuppliers, the customers' transportation to and from the stores, the customers' use of Ikea products in their homes (light bulbs, white goods, etc.), and, of course, the company's own activities, including stores, warehouses, all suppliers, and so forth—by a rough estimate the CO_2 emissions in 2009 amounted to around 27 million tons per year. Eighty-seven percent of this, however, is attributed to CO_2 emissions from raw material extraction, subsuppliers, and customer transportation and use. Only 13 percent, or 3.6 million tons, is attributed to Ikea's own units, suppliers of products, and goods transports. This illustrates the point that what most people consider when they look at a company's emissions may very well be only a very small part of the emissions that these companies are responsible for. You could of course argue that for a company to focus on the emissions close to home (i.e., emissions in the stores, offices, warehouses, transports, and suppliers) is probably just a publicity stunt. However, I recommend starting with your own activities, because if you want to influence others, like subsuppliers and customers, you need to set a good example yourself.

In 2006, we launched a comprehensive initiative to decrease CO_2 emissions in Ikea units. Under the headline "Ikea Goes Renewable," we sent out a memo describing the company's long-term objective: to power all Ikea units—stores, warehouses, offices, and Ikea-owned factories—with 100 percent renewable energy. Another objective was to increase energy efficiency in Ikea's own units by 25 percent. By 2008, we'd accomplished 45 percent renewable energy for heating, 20 percent in renewable electricity, and 20 percent overall energy efficiency improvement. Some within the company complained that my long-term objective of 100 percent was not realistic. But my feeling was and is that ambitious long-term targets help increase motivation and send the message that management is serious about radical improvements. Not to mention, of course, that we do not know today what possibilities tomorrow's technologies may bring.

Today, new Ikea stores and warehouses are fitted with renewable energy solutions. Examples include ground source heat pumps, air-to-air heat pumps, biomass boilers, and solar power. The company, as I write, is considering windmill projects. The Brooklyn store in New York is testing solar photo voltage for electricity production. The Swedish store in Karlstad has one of the largest geothermal installations in Sweden. The Spreitenbach store in Zurich, Switzerland, is entirely heated using wood pellets and sunshine. The Wurzburg store in Germany includes the use of under-floor heating and cooling, ground source heat pumps, and liquid biofuel.

Another area we addressed as part of our climate change initiative was business travel. In actual volume of emissions, this is a small area, but it has a high symbolic importance because all employees have a chance to contribute. We wanted to remove a substantial need for travel through the use of virtual meetings using the Web, phone, and video. In the first five months of the project, 9,000 Web meetings with 27,000 participants were conducted. Travel costs, which had been increasing by around 20 percent per year, instead dropped by 20 percent compared to the year before.

Toward Responsible Sourcing

An important factor in reducing CO_2 emissions is the sourcing strategy. Ikea is moving toward a more regional-based rather than global-based production. We anticipated higher transportation costs in the long run. In addition, the need for shorter lead times, lower incremental economy of scale advantages, and currency fluctuations all support the argument for moving production closer to the sales markets. From a transportation point of view, this is more environmentally sound. In 2009, 56 percent of the units sold in China were sourced in Asia. Within eight years, this figure is forecasted to be 85 percent. Around 40 percent of the units sold in Russia are sourced in Russia. Unfortunately, this figure has proven difficult to increase (more about that later). Ikea's production company, Swedwood, recently opened its first wholly owned factory in the United States. In 2009, 18 percent of U.S. sales were sourced from North America. The plan is to increase local sourcing in the United States to 35 percent within eight years.

Another important aspect of the company's environmental sourcing strategy is the flat pack of furniture, allowing more efficient transportation. Other initiatives include maximizing packaging capabilities, direct deliveries, filling rates in trucks, and demands on transport providers. All these steps are intended to improve the efficiency of road transports, an area in which there is much progress still to be made.

Legislation regarding truck standards, fuel standards, road taxes, etc., will increase the speed of change. One significant challenge lies in the area of sea traffic, where there is a large imbalance between moving goods to and from Europe, Asia, and the United States. From Asia to Europe, a 100-percent fill rate is only 20 to 25 percent on the return journey to Asia. From Europe to the United States, a 100-percent fill rate is only 35 to 40 percent on the return leg of the trip (figures for 2008/9). Similar problems with lack of return freights are often the case with trucks moving through Europe. There is big potential for energy efficiencies to be achieved here if someone can find an appropriate solution to this issue.

Two general goals that all companies should have are to stop the transportation of air—that is, the number of empty vehicles—and to increase rail freight. Currently two major hurdles prevent progress on this front in Europe: lack of common standards within Europe (for instance, rail gauges) and lack of competition, since the railroads are often owned by the state (I might also cite lack of flexibility as another contributing factor to the current impasse).

Once solid actions are in place within your company, it's time to move the focus to suppliers and subsuppliers on the one hand

and also to look at the customers' use of your products or services in their homes and see how these can consume less energy.

In 1999, Ikea lagged behind in its environmental awareness and projects. Ten years later, the organization had reached a level of maturity, one in which sustainability is becoming truly integrated into the company's everyday business agendas and strategies. The pressure to improve no longer needs to come from the top of the organization. The motivation and willingness to improve is present everywhere. I am convinced this will make a big difference in the years to come.

This is an important point. In any wide-reaching initiative, a company will reach a crossroads when the pressure for change no longer need come from the top of the organization. This tipping point creates a fundamental shift in the organization's culture, one where throughout the company workers and managers alike accept and embrace these initiatives as part of their best business processes and plans.

The Impact of Environmentalism on Profits

What about the costs of environmental work? Will they have a negative impact on profitability? As described in the Ikea example above, there are undoubtedly some investments that have to be made in order to make progress. For instance, Ikea invested in renewable energy in stores and invested in human resources such as supplier auditors and forestry experts. Whether these expenses make sense from a profitability perspective depends on your time perspective regarding the business. In the short term, these items may show up on your balance sheet as negative ones, but in the longer-term perspective, there will be a positive return on these investments. Investing in renewable energy, for instance, may, given today's energy prices, have a slightly longer payback time than would your normal investments. But if you believe that energy prices will rise over time, this calculation will look better, and you can increase your independence from these high energy prices going forward.

When Ikea considered the money it spent on supplier auditors and forestry experts, we motivated these expenditures by citing productivity improvements in the factories and productivity gains in the use of the raw material (timber). Forestry experts not only helped Ikea trace the source of the timber used in the products, as part of living up to the code of conduct (since Ikea wants to make sure the timber is not taken from virgin forests), but they also helped Ikea improve its timber usage, getting more material out of the logs. In other words, it made us a better, more efficient producer. Auditors helped suppliers improve health and safety standards, improve production procedures and working conditions, and thus increase productivity and motivation among employees in the factories.

Apart from these basic profitability calculations, the company with a long-term perspective must add in the benefits of building trust and loyalty among customers, employees, governments, NGOs, and other stakeholders as a result of responsible environmental policies.

The purpose in providing this very detailed description of the Ikea case is to illustrate that it is only through actions that you can prove your credibility. Many companies talk in very general terms about their commitment to the environment. Credibility comes with facts. I have also discovered that credibility comes from strong values. When stakeholders see the people who represent the company act in accordance with the values they profess, the observers feel more confident that the company means what it says.

A question often debated in board rooms and management meetings is what communication strategy to follow regarding social and environmental actions. More and more companies are coming to the correct conclusion that it is better to focus communication on what has been achieved rather than on plans for the future. The next question then becomes, how aggressive should you be in communicating what you have achieved? This is less obvious. On the one hand, you don't want your employees, customers, and other stakeholders to think that you are doing less than you are. On the other hand, you don't want to be seen as blowing your own horn, motivated in your environmental work primarily by marketing gains. The most effective communication focuses on employees and other stakeholders with special interest in these issues—that is, NGOs and governmental institutions.

It is fine to communicate not only results but also to present future objectives as long as you feel confident that you are making progress toward them. You will find that the biggest challenge is the communication with your customers, at least if you are in the consumer business. Getting their attention is difficult enough under normal circumstances, and, as previously discussed, you must come across as serious and committed toward the environment. Issuing a few press releases will not do the trick.

I suggest this:

* Don't try to say everything; focus on a few, but important, messages.
* Never talk about how well you are doing; just inform about the facts.
* Let the receiver judge if you have done enough or not.
* Be specific in your information—facts and figures.
* If possible, let others talk about your achievements; your own credibility will always be questioned.

During my time at Ikea, I always focused on the real activities rather than the communication. Possibly as a result, we were often criticized both internally and externally for not communicating enough about what we had achieved. Despite this, I still believe one should be cautious with external communication. Social and environmental responsibility should be as evident a contribution to society as paying taxes—and most companies don't communicate to their customers how much in taxes they pay. The most important thing is that you are sincere and are seen to be so.

Charities

Other boardroom questions often debated are the policy on charity and cooperation with NGOs. I've been guided by four important principles in this regard:

- Focus
- Connection to the business
- Involvement
- Cost efficiency

Focusing your sponsorship on a few NGOs where the company becomes an important contributor gives you the possibility to influence and develop a strong partnership. Prioritize areas connected to the business (e.g., child labor is a problem in the area of carpet production). By doing that, you are more likely to have your own staff on the ground connected to the projects. NGOs appreciate personal involvement, not just money. It gives you the opportunity to engage your own employees, who will be motivated and proud of the company's contribution to society. Look for projects that are cost efficient and where you touch many lives. Prioritize projects that help the individuals become self-reliant and employable.

There has been a big increase in social and environmental actions among companies in recent years. Even so, I believe we are seeing only the beginning of this trend. The Earth's population is still growing fast. Living conditions are also improving in many developing countries. This will continue to increase the pressure on the use of our scarce resources. Progress is slow in relation to what is needed, and as the likelihood of serious environmental damage increases over the coming years, we will see more pressure for faster actions. I think it is wise for companies to have aggressive agendas today in order to meet rising expectations from society tomorrow.

CHAPTER 5

The Market Perspective

Let us change the perspective for a moment. Instead of looking at what market shares, sales, and profit companies can get from the countries they operate in, let us see how a company can add value in a specific market. Let's consider the example of Ikea's contribution in emerging markets.

1. **Offering well-designed, quality, functional, sustainable home furnishing at low prices for the middle classes.** In developing Ikea's concept of our customer base, we had to consider who wanted our product. The rising middle class has a substantial need for home furnishings. The market typically consists of imported expensive designer brands or low-quality local handicraft products.

   Ikea is perfectly placed to take advantage of this environment. With the same requirements regarding quality standards and the same level of choice of products as in the developed countries, Ikea can provide and offer unique products at substantially lower prices. In China, for instance, Ikea's prices often are 50 percent lower than in European countries.

   Ikea approached the issue of its customer base by researching how people live in their homes, trying to understand their needs and then offering solutions to those needs. Therefore, Ikea is a very interesting proposition both to consumers and governments, since the government (at least, in most countries) has an interest in raising the quality of life for its citizens. Thus, Ikea helps by making quality products.

As Western companies move into emerging markets such as China, it may be tempting to consider offering a somewhat lower quality product range, in order to be able to offer competitive prices at good margin. This is not a good approach. Offering top quality and design is the differentiator when moving to these countries. Not only does it mean providing a unique offer to the customers, this is also important to show local employees that these countries are as important as are Western markets.

Throughout its history, Ikea has shown that it is focused on customer need for quality furniture that does what the consumer wants it to do. That strengthens its appeal both in its home market and abroad.

2. **Offering employment and tax revenues.** Ikea invests in and owns both retail stores and production units. In Russia, for example, to date more than $4 billion have been invested in shopping centers, retail stores, warehouses, and production units. As well, Ikea plays a major role in exports; the company is responsible for 20 percent of all rug exports from India and is the largest furniture exporter from Russia. China accounts for more than 20 percent of all Ikea sourcing. Ikea also supports production for local use. Forty percent of all Ikea products sold in Russia are produced in Russia. More than 50 percent of the units sold in China are produced in China.

As Western companies become more and more established in emerging markets, I can sense an increasing frustration on the part of local authorities, concerns that these companies must contribute more in the areas of taxes and local production. I have some sympathy with this argument. In some cases, of course, companies accrue losses over many years while trying to establish a successful business. These losses can then be offset against profits for a number of years when the company has become profitable. It's not surprising that this can raise suspicions about some clever tax planning going on.

This, in turn, triggers reactions from tax authorities and governments that, in the eyes of Western companies, are seen as harassment. When these incidents are reported in the Western press, they are often described as examples of corruption or anticompetitive behavior. This in turn increases the division and lack of understanding between Western companies/countries and the concerned markets. A continuous open dialogue between companies and authorities concerning how to find a reasonable tax contribution is important to avoid unnecessary conflicts.

3. **Offering know-how to build a global competitive export industry.** Ikea supports suppliers with financing and practical know-how. Take the initiative to industrialize the carpet industry in India and joint ventures with furniture companies in Russia: supporting local production industry is almost always the first priority for governments in emerging markets. This is much more important to them than investments in retail stores and is probably the most important contribution to growth in developing countries that Western companies can offer.

4. **Improving social and environmental standards in production.** One of the points established at Ikea (alluded to in an earlier chapter) is that all suppliers must follow the Ikea code of conduct. We undertook more than 1,000 audits each year to ensure that compliance was consistent and ongoing. By 2009, more than 100,000 deviations had been recorded, most of which were corrected. Ikea developed projects to improve environmental standards, such as the Better Cotton Initiative in India. Members of the initiative, of which Ikea is one, educated farmers to grow cotton in an environmentally friendly way, not to use pesticides and to use much less water in the process.

Contrary to what many people in the Western world seem to think, there is great concern for the environment in emerging markets, both among governments and the general public. This provides an opportunity for companies entering these markets to set a good example and show through their actions that they care about this issue. On the other hand, both governments and suppliers have shown little interest in improving the working conditions at factories. Conventional thinking seems to be that any improvements in working conditions will jeopardize competitiveness. As I've made clear in preceding chapters, I believe this is seldom the case.

5. **The Ikea Social Initiative to improve conditions for low-income groups.** Ikea and UNICEF have an extensive partnership in India, involving projects covering 500 villages with more than one million people. Some 80,000 children are receiving an education they would otherwise have been denied.

My sense is that governments in emerging markets are having mixed feelings about companies initiating activities that can be seen as charity. On the one hand, they recognize the contributions being made, but on the other, they are concerned that education and health are government responsibilities. Working through charities or NGOs that have a good relationship with the local government is probably the best way to channel social initiatives.

A Humble, Respectful, and Long-Term Engagement

Ikea's philosophy has been to recruit and invest in local people. The company's values and management style often add a different perspective to these markets. At the same time, how the company thinks about people, leadership, and management is sometimes confusing and creates curiosity, motivation, and new learning opportunities for local managers. Ikea typically builds long-term relationships with suppliers, and this contributes to developing competences among the supplier base.

The Example of India

Let's consider the case of India. For the poorest people in the country, Ikea is providing education and health care in cooperation with UNICEF. This help prepares them to enter the job market. For the people working in low-income jobs, Ikea supports them by improving conditions at the suppliers through the company's code of conduct. Regarding the middle class, Ikea is supporting them by offering good home furnishing products at reasonable prices (in India, this will be possible as soon as foreign ownership rules are eased). For entrepreneurs, Ikea supports its suppliers and thus contributes to more jobs and global competitiveness. Throughout the environment, Ikea stresses innovation that is in the interests of the population. For example, the company supports new ways of growing cotton that will decrease the use of pesticides and reduce the use of limited water resources (i.e., the Better Cotton Initiative referred to on page 51).

Ikea's involvement in India shows how a company can contribute to a better society by touching many different groups of people in a given country.

Expand Global Contributions

To be successful, global companies must think hard about how they can contribute in a more significant way than they have been used to. Simply offering employment and (sometimes) paying taxes to a country's government is no longer enough. Global companies have a much more important role to play, making a real difference and contributing to a better society. The old saying "The business of business is business" implies that the state is solely responsible for social and environmental development. This sentiment is outdated.

The two main challenges of mankind are poverty and the environment. *These can be tackled successfully only if business, governments, and civil society work hand in hand.* Delivering products that help improve the lives of the many, combined with sustainable job creation, is the best way to tackle poverty. Jobs that provide dignity, respect, and a decent life for employees, jobs that contribute to the long-term growth and competitiveness of developing countries, make an equally important contribution. The environmental challenges will best be tackled by businesses that help their customers, suppliers, and other stakeholders to become sustainable. Any company wanting to operate in emerging markets will be immensely more successful if it embraces these higher objectives rather than just thinking about how to maximize profits. If you do, the likelihood of sustainable profitability will increase.

PART 2

Differentiation through Control of the Value Chain

n this section, I will explain the makings of a successful business model—the components of the model, the importance of entrepreneurial behavior in developing it, and how the business model connects to the vision and values. I will also illustrate the challenges of transforming a company from a small entrepreneurial to a big global business and the challenges of staying on track with a successful business model.

In many retail sectors, the norm is that product development and brand ownership are controlled by other companies than those owning the retail outlets. This is the case in big sectors like electronics, white goods, food, and DIY. In the apparel and home furnishing sectors, some retailers are in control of both brands and retail outlets. Because of this division of "power" between brand owners and retailers, the differences in the product range, prices, service, and store experience between retailers are almost undetectable to most consumers. Evidently, the key to profitability and success is differentiation. Many retailers are struggling to achieve this and end up in a situation where they survive on small margins through either being a little bit better at doing the same thing as everyone else or achieving some marginal advantage through better retail locations. Innovations in the retail industry are often easy to copy, and potential differentiation is short lived. Substantial success can, in my opinion, be achieved only when a retailer has a unique product range and is in control of the whole value chain from product development and production through to the retail outlets. The trend at the moment is definitely going in this direction. More and more retailers are developing their own brands, and I believe we will see a reduction of mid- and low-price brands owned by fast moving consumer goods companies (FMCGs). Primarily, premium brands from FMCGs will remain in demand among retailers in the longer-term perspective.

One company that has achieved control of the whole value chain is Ikea, and this is one of the key reasons to the company's success.

Establishing a Successful Business Model

Ikea spent 30 years, from 1943 to 1972, developing its business model before starting its expansion abroad. In today's world, most companies have started, flourished, and died in the time it took Ikea to get out of the starting blocks. By comparison, Walmart, the world's biggest retail company, started its business around the same time as Ikea (1945) and is today 18 times bigger in sales. Microsoft was founded in 1975 and is around two times bigger. Google started in 1998 and in only 10 years reached a sales level on par with Ikea.

Why Did It Take So Long?

Perhaps it was a sign of the times. Ikea is a Swedish company; Sweden represents a small market, quickly saturated by a successful company. Expansion abroad is the only option for continued growth. However, back in those days, global expansion was not such an easy undertaking. Conditions for global business have improved dramatically in the past 20 years. This probably partly explains why a company such as Walmart could grow faster at an earlier stage in its development, having such a huge home market compared to Ikea.

Another reason it took so long has to do with the type of industry within which Ikea is operating. Home furnishing is a very stable business compared to many others. A chair has looked pretty much the same for the past few hundred years. The industry and competition have experienced very little development. In fact, most innovation in the home furnishing retail sector has been driven by Ikea. This made it possible for the company to develop at its own pace with little pressure from outside.

But the most important explanation, I think, lies in the DNA of the company. Ikea has a very conservative financing policy—earn your money before you spend it. Growth is important, but you should take good care of your customers before you add new ones (i.e., new stores and markets). Development comes from listening to and learning from your customers, not from a quick-fix copy of what the competition is doing.

Finally, of course, all growth so far has been organic. Ikea has been reluctant to grow through acquisition and merger with other companies. With a strong culture and specific needs in terms of store size and location, it is very difficult to find a suitable company to acquire. I think it is fair to say that Ikea is not in a hurry. This may seem like a contradiction, given the track record of fast growth over many years.

How Did the Idea and Business Model Develop?

Ikea started with a traveling salesman who sold matches and developed this business into a mail order enterprise selling everything from watches to pencils. Finally the company ended up as a global home furnishing concern that sold everything for the home through stores in all corners of the world.

The process leading up to this conclusion is, of course, to a large extent a consequence of the character of Ingvar Kamprad. Many would agree that probably all elements of what today is called the Ikea culture are in fact the values and characteristics of Kamprad himself.

Cost consciousness, determination, willpower, striving to meet reality, daring to be different, a constant desire for renewal, the importance of being on the way, fellowship, and enthusiasm—all these are examples of the values that have shaped Ikea and are constantly reiterated in internal company literature and training programs. The history of these early days is well documented and plays a fundamental role in shaping and forming the spirit and value system of the organization and its employees.

Shaping of the Ikea Business Model

Furniture entered into the company's product range in 1950. This happened, simply enough, because the area around Älmhult (where Ikea was established) had many furniture producers. To sell furniture, you needed a place to show it; consequently, the mail-order business was complemented by stores when the first furniture showroom was established in Älmhult in 1953.

Furniture was bulky and therefore expensive to ship, so the solution was to introduce flat-packed furniture. By this method, transport damages and logistical costs were reduced, and another element of the Ikea concept was introduced.

In 1961, Ikea with its low prices became a threat too big to ignore for the Swedish furniture dealers, and pressure was put on manufacturers to boycott Ikea. As a consequence, Ikea found new sourcing alternatives outside the Swedish borders in Poland, thus establishing global sourcing as another fundamental part of the Ikea concept.

In 1965, the Kungens Kurva store, on the outskirts of Stockholm, was opened. This marked the introduction of a number of important cornerstones of the Ikea concept, such as big stores outside city centers with free parking. The success of the opening impelled management to open up the warehouse and let the customers pick their own merchandise: thus the self-serve warehouse was born. This also marked a move away from only furniture and introduced accessories—everything for the home—into the company's product range. There were, to be sure, other factors, but these are some of the major elements that shaped the company's business model. The point here is that the company's growth was not strictly planned but proceeded by taking advantage of opportunities as they presented themselves.

What Made This Business Model Successful?

When considering the events that shaped the company, two things stand out:

* The ability to handle challenges and problems
* The willingness to take risks

The defining moments in Ikea's history occurred when challenges turned into opportunities. I've mentioned some examples dating to the very beginning, but there are also more recent cases, such as the environmental and social challenges in the nineties that also reshaped the company in many ways.

The willingness to take risks is of course a hallmark of all great entrepreneurs, and Ikea is no exception. Moving sourcing to Poland in the fifties is one example. Investing in a giant store in the Swedish capital Stockholm in the sixties, based only on the experience of a small store in the small town of Älmhult, probably was one of the biggest financial risks the company has ever taken. A more recent example of risk taking was when the company entered the Russian market in the middle of the financial crises in the late nineties.

The ability to turn problems into new opportunities, try out new things, and take substantial risks to realize these opportunities has created a substantial distance between Ikea and its competition. Through redefining the business, not just doing things the same way but better than the competition, the company created competitive advantages. By doing things differently, companies can establish a unique position in the market, one on which they can thrive for a long time.

Ikea turned the conventional business model upside down. At the time when the Ikea concept was developed in the fifties and sixties, the furniture and home furnishing business was conservative and fragmented.

- The furniture business provided very traditional design, while Ikea presented a modern Scandinavian style.
- The furniture business targeted primarily older, established households; Ikea focused on families with children.
- The furniture business consisted of smaller specialist shops, while Ikea built big stores with everything for the home in one place.
- The furniture business was located in the city centers, yet Ikea built stores in out-of-town locations with free parking.

- The furniture business sold pieces, and Ikea offered complete solutions for the home through room sets in the stores and in the catalog.
- The furniture business did its marketing through advertising, while Ikea introduced the catalog, distributed free to all households in the catchment area.
- The furniture business offered personal service, but Ikea introduced the self-serve concept.
- The furniture business focused on the high-price segment, and Ikea focused on low prices.
- The furniture business offered ready-assembled furniture pieces, while Ikea introduced flat-pack furniture with self assembly.
- The furniture business produced locally; Ikea started very early with global sourcing.
- The furniture business sold predominantly supplier models, and Ikea developed its own range.

Five Components of Distinction

By setting itself apart from the competition, Ikea started to create a distinct and unique brand, different from everyone else. Through this development of the business model, the competitive advantages in the eyes of the customers started to take shape.

Why do customers choose Ikea over other retailers? What are the customer needs that Ikea satisfies?

- Design, function, and quality at low prices
- Unique (Scandinavian) design
- Inspiration, ideas, and complete solutions
- Everything in one place
- "A day out," the shopping experience

These five success criteria come across as very basic solutions to customer needs. You may well say that they are similar to those of most companies. The difference, in my opinion, is that Ikea is much better at delivering on these customer needs than are other retailers. The company's business model represents a blueprint for how they are executed.

Most competitors focus on one or at most two of these customer needs. High-street shops focus on design and inspiration. Out-of-town low-cost retailers focus on price. Department stores focus on choice. The real strength of Ikea lies in the combination of all five. Adding them together makes the company unique and relevant to its customers.

Now let us take a brief look at these five components. (They will be discussed in more detail in the following chapter).

Design, Function, and Quality at Low Prices

The most important strength of the company is the ability to deliver good design, function, and quality at really low prices. Ikea has an obsession with low prices. The internal goal is to always have prices at least 20 percent below the competition on comparable products, and often even more than that. For instance, between 1999 and 2009, we strove to reduce prices by 20 percent. The intention of the current leadership is to keep on reducing them going forward.

Key to this is the integrated process of production-adapted product development together with the suppliers, global sourcing, the distribution idea of flat pack, and the integration of the customer in the selection, distribution, and assembly of the products. Also important to the success of the company is a strong focus on cost consciousness and, of course, big sales volumes, creating buying price advantages.

Through this, Ikea manages to combine low prices, good quality, and profitability.

The Unique Scandinavian Design

Ikea sought to develop its own unique range with a Scandinavian/Swedish style. This design element was even more unique in the seventies when the international expansion started.

You can choose to adapt your company's product range to the markets you are operating in, or you can choose to shift the market's preference toward your own range and style. Ikea has chosen the latter. By doing this, the company can maintain a unique and distinct profile. This is, however, a more difficult path to follow. Changing people's taste remains one of the biggest challenges to growth in many of Ikea's markets.

Inspiration, Ideas, and Solutions

A third competitive advantage is the ability to provide inspiration, ideas, and solutions to the customers' home furnishing needs. For example, Ikea shows room sets in the stores and in the catalog. This is an area where Ikea is still well ahead of the competition. It is also difficult to copy because to achieve it, companies need real home furnishing competence. A significant understanding of the customer's situation at home is the basis for Ikea's product development and the creation of the main media through which the product is presented to the public—the store, the Internet, and the catalog .

Everything under One Roof

To provide everything for your home in one place is, of course, a point of difference between Ikea and specialty stores. The average Ikea store being built today is around 35,000 square meters and has around 8,500 different products. This is a significant increase from around 15,000 square meters 15 years ago.

In our day and age, where time is becoming more and more valuable, the ease of shopping provided by having everything in one place is becoming more and more relevant.

The Shopping Experience

The Ikea store in Kungens Kurva has for many years now been the main tourist attraction in the Swedish capital, Stockholm. A store visit lasts on average one and a half hours. By providing a children's ball room, a restaurant, and different family activities, Ikea tries to create something more than just another shop—the company offers the whole family a fun day out.

Five Basic Customer Needs

In this way, Ikea meets five of the most important customer needs:

1. Fantastic value for money (design, function, quality at low prices)
2. Exclusive products (Scandinavian design sold only at Ikea)
3. Inspiration and ideas (solutions for your home)
4. Ease of shopping (everything in one place, take home direct)
5. Fun (a day out)

The fact that these components are so simple is a strength. No matter how our society will develop in coming years, people will always have these needs. These needs are relevant to almost any business, not just retail. The challenge, of course, will always be how to continue deliver on them in a way that's better than the competition.

Let me reiterate this point: *satisfying a variety of basic customer needs, and doing so in a better way than the competitors, is at the core of any business success.*

The Power of Consistency

Another important factor for Ikea's success that at first glance may seem to be in conflict with differentiation is consistency. Companies frequently change the core components of their business such as their range or their target customer groups. This may, of course, be necessary when you are in trouble, but it does not help in building a strong brand identity.

The Ikea product range—its style and content, the concept and way of doing business, and the target customer groups—was developed in the fifties and sixties. Since then, the company has essentially expanded that model worldwide. The main components have remained the same. Continuous reevaluation of the different components of the business model/concept and their relevance and then gradual adaptation—evolution rather than revolution—has been the name of the game.

There are many reasons why this has been possible.

- Ikea is not a listed company and can work from a more long-term perspective.
- Having the same owner during all these years creates continuity.
- The company recruits the highest levels of management internally, which ensures stability and understanding of the criteria for success.
- Ikea is in a very stable line of business compared to, for instance, the telecom industry.
- A real point of difference was created early on that has been nourished, developed, and kept relevant during all these years.

Ikea's success has grown from stability and consistency regarding the big picture but with lots of action and innovation in the detail. Once the company established the concept, evolution rather than revolution became the Ikea way to build a strong brand identity.

That the Ikea brand is bigger than the company's actual size is shown by the fact that in 2007 Ikea was ranked only number 37 in sales among all retail companies. However, in terms of brand recognition, the ranking was number 38 among all global brands and first among retail companies, as reported by Interbrand, published in *BusinessWeek*.

What this story tells us is how real transformation of the conventional business model in combination with taking charge of the entire value chain can give companies a long-term advantage. To make it happen, you need strong company values and an owner willing to take risks and promote long-term thinking.

The Successful Entrepreneur

The development of the Ikea business model, in my mind, is a very good example of classic entrepreneurship. By "entrepreneurship," I mean focusing on opportunities that are derived from problems that need a solution. The bigger and more difficult, the better. Very often these opportunities are revenue driven—the focus is growth. Entrepreneurship is about a willingness to take substantial risk to realize these opportunities and about having a long-term perspective on the work. This perspective is fundamental to making the right decisions. Entrepreneurship is about being motivated by strong visions and values and understanding their importance to the business. It would seem to me that this is the most successful way of developing any business, entrepreneurial or otherwise. I think many companies would benefit from more entrepreneurial behavior.

In the following section, I will illustrate in more depth how companies can achieve differentiation in product range and price. I will also discuss the challenges of integrating the different parts of the value chain effectively.

CHAPTER 6

Creating a Unique Product Range

The product range is at the core of any retail company. Being able to differentiate in range and price versus the competition is more important than any other aspect of retailing. Location, services, store standards, etc., are all important, but they are secondary to having an attractive product offering. Range differentiation is a major challenge in many retail sectors, such as food, DIY, or electronics, where the major brands are developed and owned by other companies further back in the value chain.

Ikea controls the entire value chain including the product range, a factor that puts it in a good position. Both the company vision and the business idea clearly state what Ikea is about: "To create a better everyday life for the many people through offering a wide range of well designed, functional home furnishing products at prices so low that the majority of people will be able to afford them."

This really says it all. Ikea has a social ambition—to create a better everyday life for the many. The company also has a high ambition to create an offer that has all the ingredients the customer can possibly want—a lot of choice, good design, and functionality at very good prices. Anyone who can deliver on that will be a market leader.

Creating a Wide Range

Now let us look at what this business idea actually means. First of all, consider the problems of creating a wide range of products. There are many opportunities to go wrong here. In 2010, Ikea stores had more than 600 million visitors. Almost anything could probably be put into the stores and it would sell well, at least initially. And there have been many proposals to add products to the company's mix. However, the company has not let itself be tempted to stray off track; only home furnishing products are allowed into the stores. This is the area Ikea knows well and where it can create competitive prices. This way the company stays focused on delivering on its vision and business idea and maintains a clear brand profile.

Each product range area of the store (e.g., textile, kitchen, sofas) should have a selection rich enough for the customers to see Ikea as one of the best specialist shops in the area. This has become an area of great challenges. Competition has increased over the past 20 years, and there are many more alternatives, "category killers," or specialty shops with which Ikea must compete in each range area.

At the same time, many years of sales growth have increased the need for a very efficient logistical flow through the supply chain and into the stores in order to maintain a low cost level. Even though the size of an average Ikea store has increased from around 15,000 square meters in the nineties to 35,000 square meters in 2009, and even if some of the range has been put on customer order (meaning that the customers order the products in the store and get them delivered directly to the home), Ikea is still struggling to maintain a wide enough range in the stores to live up to the statement that it is one of the best specialist shops in all different range categories. The average store holds a range of around 8,500 articles. There is constant pressure to reduce this number to maintain logistical efficiency.

Accommodating these two objectives simultaneously—a competitive range in terms of choice, and efficient store logistics—is difficult. When Ikea has to prioritize between the two, it almost always chooses logistical efficiency over wider choice. At the end of the day, low costs are necessary to maintain low prices, and low prices will always be the first priority at Ikea (again using the vision and business idea as guiding principles).

The "New" Factor

Another aspect of "a wide range" is the importance of new items. Most retailers see new products as an important commercial opportunity, a way to bring more customers into the stores. However, a high renewal rate is also in conflict with logistical efficiency and low costs.

In this area, as in the width of its range, Ikea prioritizes logistical efficiency. The yearly renewal rate peaked at 30 percent but was in 2010 down to around 20 percent. This puts very high demands on the product developers to be successful in creating commercial products all the time. Low costs and low prices—again the priority is clear.

Local Appeal

Another interesting aspect of the problem of range is the question, "To what extent should the range be locally adapted?" Maintaining a single range across many countries means it will necessarily be limited, and consequently there will be bigger sales volumes for individual products, resulting in low buying prices.

Historically, the company has limited local adaptations to functional differences such as sizes of bed sheets, glasses, beds, kitchens, etc. However, from time to time there has been strong pressure from different country organizations to find more local solutions. When those demands have been accommodated, the Ikea range identity has tended to become weaker. As well, the costs (higher buying prices, logistical costs, markdown of prices) and the product availability in the stores have run out of control. In the United States, Ikea actually lost a sales opportunity because the country managers did not believe that the standard range of kitchens and wardrobes could be sold in that market (more about this later).

Again, a tight range and cost control take precedence over more choice. However, this is an area where the philosophy of the company's leadership is changing somewhat. The expansion to low-purchasing-power countries in the past decade has increased the need for more local range adaptation. More local solutions are being developed to accommodate the needs of these countries for low-price products combined with clever storage solutions for smaller homes.

Product Style

Another interesting aspect of product range is the product's style. Not surprisingly, Ikea's products are seen as Scandinavian and, within Scandinavia, as typically Swedish. The challenge here is appealing to many people while maintaining a unique identity. The appeal of Swedish design is limited outside Scandinavia.

The company's leadership has taken the position that the company must work to change the taste of people to favor the Ikea style rather than to be more like everyone else. This has proven difficult. In most countries, there is very limited change in style preferences, and the majority of people still have a traditional taste in home furnishing. This is curious, given how modern and willing to change most people are in other areas such as cars, clothes, electronics, travel, etc. But when entering young people's homes, it is surprising how often they look like the homes of the parents or even grandparents. Given the slow progress of change in taste, such factors can limit growth. Therefore the company has, very carefully, made some changes to the style of its products in an effort to make them more relevant to our customers (the vision, again).

Design and Function Are Essential

At Ikea, beautiful design is not limited to the expensive part of the product range. And it cannot be if the company intends to live up to its vision of a better everyday life for the majority of people. Design statements are made in range launches under the sub brands "PS collection," "Ikea 365+," and "Ikea Stockholm." Both PS and 365+ are positioned in the midprice range; these are products for everyday use. But of course good design must be part of *all* product development. In my opinion, Ikea still has a challenge to achieve great design in the low-priced segment of its products, something that is necessary in order to live up to the company's vision.

As well, the products must be functional. Functionality is a real trademark of Ikea and largely responsible for its strong reputation among customers. Clever solutions, added benefits, and multi-use products are strong features of the Ikea range.

At the very heart of everything Ikea does is an understanding of people's lives at home. It is the starting point of product and range development, and it is the basis for developing the room sets in the stores and catalog. The company doesn't place as its first priority that the products shall look nice. It is that they shall work for whoever lives in the home—in their everyday life. Storage solutions are Ikea's strongest area, and that is why bedroom and kitchens are the two categories with the biggest sales share in the range. Functionality together with good value for the money are, in my opinion, the two most important aspects of the success in this range. They are also in line with the company's vision to improve the life of the many.

Quality

How about quality? The business idea states, "Ikea shall have a wide range, design, functionality, and low prices," but there is no mention of quality. I sometimes wonder if this has had an impact on the reluctance to prioritize quality. Throwaway products are not characteristic of Ikea. Quality must not be an end in itself but should be adapted to the consumer's needs. This means, for example, that solid wood is not put on the back side of a drawer where that quality is of no use to the customer and would only increase the price.

All this is fine, and it helps Ikea to be clever about developing products. Historically, though, the push to reduce prices has no doubt had a negative impact on the product quality. And this relates back to customer perception of Ikea's quality.

An additional challenge to product quality perception is the fact that the customers have to assemble the products themselves. This is necessary to keep costs and sales prices low, but it puts high demands on the creativity of product designers and technicians to make assembly and assembly instructions so simple that customers can put the products together without making mistakes—mistakes they might translate into lack of product quality.

A lot of hard work has gone into improving the product quality during the last few years, but undoubtedly this is an area where there is still much to be done.

"Delivering prices so low that the many people will be able to afford them." This is the most fundamental statement that exists in Ikea's business model. Low prices take priority over everything else. Low prices are the very foundation of the vision and business idea.

The Importance of Pricing

The power of the price cannot be underestimated, but price is not randomly arrived at. It has to complement design, functionality, and a wide choice. The ability to deliver extremely good value for the money compared to its competitors is the main reason for Ikea's success. There are reasons why the company is able to get this right. One is the courage not to be too greedy on the margin. In this regard, the company believes that reducing prices substantially, not just a little, will bring rewards.

It's also important, of course, to know how to do this while making profits! For most competitors, having the lowest price seems to mean being 5 to 10 percent cheaper than the competition on comparable products. At Ikea, this means being a minimum 20 percent cheaper and often up to 50 percent cheaper than the competition. In the ten years from 1999 to 2009, prices to the customers were reduced by 20 percent on average across the range. In the Western European countries, close to 80 percent of the company's customers have said that Ikea has better prices than others. When new important products are being introduced, they can be priced at a level 50 percent or more below competition. The company's margin will initially be very low because the sales volumes are still unknown. The company's thinking is that as a consequence of the incredibly low price, competitors will not be able to follow and sales volume will rise with the consequence of better buying prices that will help drive the margin to the right level. I think this is a good example of applying courage, believing that an offensive pricing approach will deliver high sales volumes, and making the investment in the form of a lower margin up front to be able to harvest the rewards later.

How can Ikea deliver these low prices and yet be a profitable company?

Controlling the Value Chain

The secret is the control and coordination of the whole value chain from raw material, production, and range development, to distribution into stores. Most other companies working in the retail sector have control either of the retail end (stores and distribution) or the product design and production end.

Ikea's vertical integration makes it a complex company compared to most, since it owns both production, range development, distribution, and stores. It buys in more than 50 countries and sells in 28 countries. The complexity is a challenge, but it is also the big differentiator and competitive advantage the company has when it is executed in the right way.

A well-coordinated pipeline or value chain with the lowest sales price as the guiding principal for what is done delivers the results. All decisions are made with an eye toward delivering the best price. The result has been a small common range rather than a big choice with many local adaptations; logistical efficiency in the whole pipeline; range development based on deep knowledge of both the production possibilities and the customer's needs; big sales volumes; and a buying organization in many countries with substantial knowledge of where in the world to find the best production possibilities for each product category. No products are taken into the range unless they can be flat packed. The customer is an integrated part of the supply chain, choosing, paying, taking home, and assembling the products himself, thus contributing to lower prices.

The key to this pricing ability is the product development company Ikea of Sweden AB (IOS), based in Älmhult, Sweden. This organization is unknown to most outsiders, but it is of vital importance to Ikea. IOS is in charge of the product range and its coordination from supplier to customer. All the competencies of around 1,000 employees are based in the same location. This creates advantages such as transfer of knowledge, common working methods, and common IT systems. It facilitates succession planning across functions and range areas. Internally, it's common to have discussions about the size of this organization and the problems of recruiting people to live in the small town of Älmhult, far from major cities. At various times, the company has debated if parts or all of IOS should be relocated. Doing so is perhaps not in the company's best interests. After all, one of the secrets of Ikea's success is its heritage and Swedish background.

Setting Commercial Priorities

I close this chapter with a final reflection on the product range—how to decide on the commercial priorities. Having a broad range with everything for the home means making choices when deciding what to prioritize. As I mentioned earlier, the stores pose a limitation regarding how many articles they can carry, and the marketing budget poses another limitation concerning what to communicate in external media. Historically, the organization has given every range area equal attention and resources. In consequence, sales growth has been fairly even across range areas.

Back in 2004, this strategy was changed. The idea was to focus on the two strongest range areas, bedrooms and kitchens, and decisively move them to a new sales level. These two areas should form the growth engine for the existing stores in all markets. These two areas alone contributed 40 percent of Ikea's total sales. These are also the areas with the biggest advantage both in the supply chain and in the eyes of customers. It was decided that over a period of at least three years, these two areas would be given more marketing consideration at the expense of some other areas; they would get more space in the stores and more space in the catalog. They would get more external marketing money, more investment in rebuilding their areas in the stores, investment in coworker training, extended service offering, and investments in better IT support systems. And above all, investments in reduced sales prices on key products would be substantial.

Already, within the first year of the initiative, the bedroom range was pacing at a growth rate of 20 percent in comparable stores. Continuing through to the next two years, both bedroom and kitchen were reaching sales growth levels far above other range areas. Contrary to fears, there was no corresponding decline in sales in the other range areas.

Ikea is better at building long-term advantages and creating stronger growth when prioritizing and focusing on fewer areas. History has shown many times that this strategy pays off.

In this chapter, I have tried to illustrate some of the important aspects of building a unique product range and how a powerful vision and business idea can successfully guide the decision making and development of a company product offer when tough choices have to be made. Most retailers are struggling with the potential conflict between, on the one hand, offering a very price-competitive range while remaining profitable, which in most cases has the consequence of a limited range or choice, lower quality, little renewal or new products, and a standardization across many markets or less adaptation to local conditions and, on the other hand, an attractive range with much to choose from, high quality, and a high degree of new products locally adapted to each market's need, which drives a high cost structure and thus higher consumer prices.

Neither of these extremes seems to be very successful. The preferred way of reaching a good balance of price competitiveness, profitability, and an attractive product offer is to control the entire value chain to achieve unique products and prices and establish a product range big enough for your company to be perceived as a specialist in your given line of business. How big this range is will depend mainly on the competitive situation. The necessary rate of product renewal and local market adaptation depend mainly on what business sector and what markets you are operating in.

CHAPTER 7

Building a Supply Chain to Deliver Low Prices

If the product range is where the point of difference regarding the offer is established, the supply chain is where much of the price competitiveness and profitability are created. The key to being successful in this area is the ability to control the entire supply chain from production to the retail outlets.

Importance of the Buying Organization

Together with the stores, the buying organization has always been the part of Ikea that holds the highest status. This can be explained partly by the impact the buying organization has had on the price competitiveness of the company and partly by the Ikea culture where "being close to reality," "being in the frontline," and learning from the shop floor and suppliers are fundamental principles of the company. The store managers and buyers were and are the heroes of the company.

The importance of the buying organization was established back in the beginning of the 1960s when Ikea moved much of its buying to Poland. The ability to reduce purchase prices by 50 percent or more practically overnight had an enormous impact on the company. The Ikea sales price advantage was established, and at the same time the company made good profits. Back then, in the communist era, most production in Eastern Europe was exported to Russia or other Eastern Bloc countries. When Ikea entered the scene, Poland saw an opportunity to export to the West. Ikea also had the advantage of being first among Western companies to source its products from Eastern Europe and could benefit from the good purchase prices.

This was a difficult environment to work in. Government central planning organizations made all the decisions with little business knowledge, and their competence in furniture production was limited. However, Ikea managed to build up a sizable sourcing share in Eastern Europe in the seventies and eighties that contributed significantly to the low sales prices and profitability of the company. However, a lack of competence and resources among Eastern European suppliers, combined with Ikea's then less-than-perfect internal work processes and coordination, led to problems with product quality and product availability. In the seventies and eighties, Ikea established an unfortunate reputation for poor quality and out-of-stock products that would take many years to improve.

When the Berlin Wall fell in 1989, the situation changed. The state subsidies disappeared, and the Eastern European currencies, formerly pegged to the Russian ruble, lost their value. The supplier prices skyrocketed, and a new purchasing strategy was needed.

Two very important sourcing policies of Ikea up to that point were that the company should never own production itself, and the company should never have a too-significant share of any suppliers' production. The reason was evident: Ikea wanted to keep the flexibility to easily reduce or move production when needed, and the company wanted to hedge the risk of losing all production on key articles, should a supplier suddenly lose its production capabilities, such as to fire or bankruptcy. These policies were abandoned in the nineties for good reasons.

Sourcing Strategies

The new sourcing strategy of the nineties was characterized by four main points.

1. Move production to new low cost countries, predominantly in Asia.
2. Reduce the number of suppliers significantly.
3. Place a stronger focus on reducing purchasing prices, and increase competition between buying offices.
4. Start Ikea-owned production with the acquisition of the company Swedwood.

Move production to new low cost countries, predominantly in Asia. The push to increase buying from Asia was important and had a big impact on purchase prices. Buying offices were established in China, India, Pakistan, Bangladesh, Vietnam, Malaysia, Thailand, and Indonesia. The success in these countries was mixed. The big engine was, and still is, China.

By 2000, 22 percent of all Ikea buying came from Asia, and approximately half of that, or 10 percent of the total, came from China. Ten years later, in 2009, 30 percent of all Ikea buying came out of Asia, and two-thirds of that 30 percent, or 20 percent of the total, originated from China. So far, very little furniture is sourced in Asia, so the share of the fast-moving products coming from Asia is very high in some product categories.

In 2000, China and Poland alone contributed with almost 20 percent of all Ikea sourcing. Ten years later, in 2009, that figure was almost 40 percent. These two countries are incredibly important to Ikea. And I am sure their contribution will increase even more in the future.

Reduce the number of suppliers significantly. The reduction of the number of suppliers was a second important shift in strategy in the nineties. In 1990, Ikea sales revenues were $3.9 billion (€2.7 billion) with around 2,500 suppliers. In 2009, the size of the range was the same, but sales had reached $31.4 billion (€21.5 billion) with only 1,220 suppliers. This translated to 10 times more sales and half the number of suppliers—a remarkable change in just 20 years.

This, of course, meant abandoning the earlier principal of not having a too-significant share with any individual supplier. Today, there are many suppliers with 100 percent or close to 100 percent

Ikea production. This involves some risks, but they are risks worth taking. The advantage for the company is not only greater buying volumes and, as a consequence, lower prices, but also efficiency gains in logistics, transports, productivity, and quality control.

Place a stronger focus on reducing purchasing prices, and increase competition between buying offices. The third element of the strategy was more of a mixed blessing. It helped reduce prices, to be sure. All incentive systems, key figures, and follow up systems were primarily focused on reducing purchase prices. The competition between offices was very motivating for many employees in the buying organization. But it did lead to some negative suboptimization. Product availability, quality, logistical costs, and packaging didn't improve sufficiently. It was evident that doing one thing very well didn't always give the best overall result.

Focus and priority are always good, but sometimes the issues at hand are too many and too complex and need to be addressed in an integrated systematic way to get the best overall result. I will return to this issue shortly.

Start Ikea-owned production with the acquisition of the company Swedwood. The fourth important element of the strategy was the introduction of the company's own production through the Swedwood Group. Since the acquisition in 1991, Swedwood has grown to a production value of $1.7 billion (€1.2 billion) with 15,000 employees working in 46 production units (2009). The Swedwood Group was in 2009 responsible for close to 15 percent of the total Ikea buying volume.

Why did Ikea start its own production? There are three reasons.

1. In some key furniture production areas, Ikea has simply become too big to find suitable external producers.
2. In two of the most important product categories, board and solid wood products, there are some production methods that the company wants to protect and thus keep in-house.
3. With Swedwood, Ikea has a reference, a good example and standard setter for other suppliers. Swedwood has also become

an in-house competence center for new development in both materials and production techniques.

Overall, there is no doubt that Swedwood has been a success story. With their support, Ikea has been able to increase its lead on the competition in primarily board-based furniture.

Ultimately, the nineties brought the Ikea supply chain thinking forward in some important areas. The move to low price countries in Asia, the reduction of the supplier base, and the introduction of its own production company Swedwood all represented important steps forward for Ikea. The problems with increasing buying prices due to changes in external factors—in this case, the fall of the Berlin Wall—were again turned into new opportunities that would reduce the buying prices even more.

Sharpening the Supply Chain

By 2000, there was still some potential for further price gains by moving more production to Asia; there was also more potential to reduce the supplier base. But more was needed to live up to the ambitions in the "Ten Jobs in Ten Years" strategy. The company's ambition was to continue reducing sales prices by 20 percent in the next 10 years. Consequently, this needed to be financed with a further 20 percent reduction in buying prices.

Again, a new strategy was needed to further sharpen the supply chain. But this time, it wasn't enough to reduce the prices. The company also needed to make substantial improvements in product availability, logistics, product quality, and, not least, to take on the challenge of improving environmental and social conditions at the suppliers.

Even though there had been some very good development in buying prices, there were further challenges. Surprisingly, given the fact that Ikea has one common range, one common distribution organization, and one common buying organization, there was a big disconnect in the supply chain. Range development, distribution, buying, and retail markets lived separate lives. The company was, and always had been, functionally organized. Goals and objectives were not coordinated, and work processes, time plans, and IT systems were built up in isolation in the different functions. The buying organization prioritized the purchase price at the supplier. The stores wanted frequent deliveries, no damages, and good product availability. The distribution organization wanted full trucks and good transport economy. The buying organization, which needed a long-term perspective to build up supplier capacity, had to guess what to buy because range development had a shorter planning cycle. The retailers planned their commercial activities with limited coordination with the supply chain.

The result of all this was increasing frustration and lack of trust between the different functions. Some of the positive effects of better purchasing prices at the supplier were then being offset by higher distribution costs, damages, quality issues, and increased handling costs in the stores. Most important, however, the availability of products in the stores had not improved.

With this in mind, the company took on the challenge of changing all this through a new supply strategy. This strategy was built on optimizing the total supply chain rather than its parts. The new common objectives for the supply chain became:

- The total supply costs, including purchase price at the supplier, distribution costs, and transport costs
- Product availability
- Product quality
- Social and environmental responsibility at the suppliers

Transforming the Ikea supply chain from a functional organization to a process-oriented one, with all that it entailed—a common supply chain strategy, a new organizational setup, new working methods and IT systems—was probably one of the biggest changes the company had ever undertaken.

The distribution organization—including warehousing, transportation, supply planning, and logistics—was merged with the buying organization into one supply-chain organization. From that point, all work procedures needed to be changed from a functional to a process-oriented approach, requiring all supply-related work processes to be coordinated from the supplier end to the retail end. As a consequence of this, the company needed to change all IT systems supporting the supply chain. This meant altering hundreds of IT systems and applications. The change also included new common objectives and financial steering of the supply chain to support the common agenda. This meant thousands of employees needed to change attitudes, change behaviors, and retrain with new IT support systems. This change needed to take place at the same time as the company grew by 10 to 15 percent per year and reduced purchase prices by 20 percent over the 10-year period.

The Right Time Frame

From the start to its eventual finish, this transformation will have taken more than 10 years. Many have wondered if this could have been done quicker with a different focus and priority. On the margin, of course, things could have been done differently and perhaps better, but overall, it is wise to tread carefully with a project of this magnitude. For one thing, the priority must always be that the supply chain works without interruption every day. Small step changes are less risky than big leaps.

Secondly, you learn an awful lot during the change process. You find that you want to integrate changes in the system as you proceed, rather than going back and changing them later. I do not think it is wise to put all your best resources into projects for the future, since you also need to produce results today.

Finally, many of the benefits of a change like this are accrued during the change phase, so speeding up the transformation to get it finished is not necessary to start seeing the benefits.

New Supply Strategy

This transformation of the supply chain was the main part of the new supply strategy, but it also included a number of other components. As earlier discussed, the company continued the move to Asia while reducing suppliers. The Asian share grew from 22 percent to 30 percent from 2000 to 2009, and the number of suppliers continued to decrease from 2,000 to 1,200 during the 10 years of the plan.

The company also pushed to increase direct deliveries from suppliers to stores as a way to decrease supply costs. The share of direct deliveries increased from around 25 percent to almost 40 percent by 2009. Larger sales volumes and bigger stores made this possible.

Ikea also shifted its distribution strategy. Until recently, all central warehouses were carrying the full range (excluding direct delivered range). In the new strategy, the slow-moving range represents about 10 percent of sales, but 50 percent of the articles are held in one or two low flow central warehouses that serve all of Europe. The fast-moving range representing 50 percent of the sales volume is stored in warehouses close to the markets. That way it is possible to better combine full transportation loads with frequent deliveries to the stores. As well, security stock could be reduced by holding slow-moving products in only one or two locations.

A further focus has been to improve the store logistics. Reducing the number of movements of products in the stores has been the biggest contributor to better productivity over a number of years.

Finally, another big change has been the introduction of more ready-to-sell packaging where the entire range has been revisited to improve packaging solutions. This again has reduced the number of hours needed in the stores.

All these changes are examples of a more integrated supply chain where the different parts work together toward common objectives.

To create new price advantages, Swedwood has moved toward more backward integration. From initially having only furniture factories, they have taken control over the raw materials, saw mills, board suppliers, and component factories. This backward integration helps Ikea gain new benefits in the production chain where the use of raw materials, production, and transports can be better optimized.

Growing the retail business in countries such as the United States, Russia, Japan, and China has also increased the need for local sourcing. There is now a movement from global to more regional sourcing with the ambition to increase the share sourced in Asia for sales in Asia and likewise for North America and Russia.

Other important shifts in the strategy are the improved coordination of purchases across different product categories. Better coordination of range development, both across different range areas and coordination with supply planning, is giving Ikea new opportunities to reduce purchase prices. Again, the integrated supply chain is creating new possibilities.

Bringing Social Issues to the Fore

Another big shift in the supply strategy, which started in 2000, was Ikea's new focus on responsibility for environmental and social issues. The concern for the environment and working conditions at suppliers in the developing world was and still is an increasing concern among customers and other stakeholders. Given that Ikea wants to live up to its vision and be seen as a responsible company, it was necessary to take a firm stand on this and become a leading example in social and environmental work. Internally, this move initially met with skepticism.

- Was there really any negative impact on the world we live in?
- Was this really the responsibility of business rather than governments?
- Do employees and customers really care?
- What right does Ikea have to put demands on the suppliers?
- Will the costs endanger the profitability and ultimately the survival of the company?

The questions were many. At the retail end of the business, employees were generally positive toward this change, but in the buying organization, there was reluctance, especially in the Far East organization.

In the end, the new ambitions prevailed, and in 2000 the company introduced a new code of conduct, one that specifies the minimum requirements placed on suppliers and describes what they can then expect from Ikea in return. This code is presented in more detail in Chapter 4.

Strict policies against child labor. One of the most important aspects of this strategy is the prevention of child labor at the suppliers and their subcontractors. In 2000, Ikea joined forces with UNICEF to prevent and eliminate child labor in the carpet belt in northern India. Up until 2015, Ikea will support UNICEF projects in India with a total amount of around $219 million (€150 million). This makes the company the biggest contributor to UNICEF within the business community.

Today, Ikea's social and environmental agenda is an integral part of the supply chain strategy.

Conclusion

In conclusion, I think it is fair to say that the Ikea supply chain has moved with the times. Benefited from global sourcing very early on in Eastern Europe, but then when that advantage disappeared with the fall of the Berlin Wall in 1989, Ikea quickly found new possibilities with the move to suppliers in Asia, the reduction in number of suppliers, and the introduction of its own production company. With the never-ending push to find new ways to reduce buying prices even further while also tackling other fundamental issues such as product availability, product quality, and environmental and social issues, Ikea took on the big task of changing the supply chain from a functional to a process-oriented organization, which unlocked new opportunities. Purchase price was reduced another 20 percent between 2000 and 2009, as had been set out in the "Ten Jobs" strategy. The company has passed the point of no return in transforming the supply chain organization, and it's reaching the end of the IT restructuring. Real improvements in the availability of products in the stores have been achieved.

It is a testament to the new supply chain strategy that Ikea passed the test of handling the financial crisis in 2008 when the company managed to quickly adapt the inventory level and keep good product availability to customers during the sudden sales drop in the autumn of 2008. Without the new process-oriented setup, this would not have been possible. There are still plenty of possibilities to change processes, and there are some challenges ahead, of course.

An Efficient Supply Chain Is Core to All Retail Companies

Only the best can be competitive on price and profitability. What the Ikea story regarding its supply chain and its development from the 1960s up until today has taught me is the importance of major decisive moves to reach new substantial advantages. These include:

* The move to Poland and Eastern Europe in the sixties
* The move to Asia and the introduction of its own production (Swedwood) in the nineties
* The transformation of the supply chain from a functional to a process-oriented organization and the move to improve conditions at the suppliers in the first decade of the twenty-first century

Small, incremental changes are good, but it is the big shifts with investments, risk taking, and a long-term view that make the difference. To achieve that, you need guidance from your vision and values, and you need owners who are prepared to make the investments and take the necessary risk.

CHAPTER 8

Efficient Retail Stores

The task of the retail store is to combine a high level of inspiration and commerciality and an exciting and smooth shopping experience—and at the same time be a very cost-efficient sales machine. These high standards need to be kept up consistently during long opening hours seven days a week. To be able to compete on prices and maintain a profitable business, retailers must be better than the competition at operating efficient stores.

The Challenges of Growth

Over the years, Ikea stores have increased substantially in size. Let's look at some of the numbers. Sales of $140 million (€100 million) per year are not unusual. Stores are open 60 to 70 hours a week. Most of them have 500 plus employees, and staff fluctuation can be between 4 percent and 80 percent a year. More than 50 percent of these store employees have less than two years of experience. More than 50 percent work part-time. More than 2 million visitors per year pass through an average store. Customer service expectations have increased over the years, and the pressure to reduce costs is higher than ever before.

Meanwhile, staff costs have grown to 40 percent of the total cost base of an Ikea store. Increasing store productivity is essential to improve the overall cost level and to continue delivering low prices. The challenge during the 10 years 1999 to 2009 was the imbalance between reduced sales prices and increased salary costs. Sales prices were reduced on average 2 percent per year while at the same time salaries increased by some 3 percent on average per year. This required around a 5 percent productivity increase every year just to stay at the same cost level. The company achieved this level of productivity, but an 8 to 10 percent productivity increase was needed to improve the cost base. This has proven very hard to achieve so far given the challenges of improving store standards, longer opening hours, and higher service requirements.

So what are some of the key strategies needed to achieve the task of operating a retail store—combining high standards with increased productivity? Primarily, all parts of a retail company must be focused on setting the right conditions for the stores. Again, this is an example of where working as one company rather than suboptimizing the parts has its advantages. Simplifying the store operations must be a key priority for all parts of the organization. Secondly, customers must be even more integrated in the sales process, doing more themselves while having the perception of an improved service level. Thirdly, the stores must be focused on people management. And fourthly, the store must relentlessly work on improving standards and operational excellence through benchmarking.

Standardization of Solutions

Setting the right conditions for the store involves a number of things—standardization of sales solutions, logistical work processes that minimize the movement and handling of products in the store, and the use of technology and IT to further simplify work procedures. Looking at the Ikea example, standardizing sales solutions is a fairly recent phenomenon. Back in the 1990s, most sales solutions were developed in isolation in every retail country. There were no global resources coordinating this. Today, practically every sales solution in the store is standardized, such as the layout and size of the sales areas, room sets, materials used, and equipment. There are also very specific standards for sales steering—that is, what products to promote and how to do it. The work to improve the logistics of the store has been one of the main cornerstones within Ikea to improve productivity and product availability in the last 10 years. I would even say that this is the main reason for the 5 percent productivity increase per year that has been achieved. One priority has been to move all products directly from arrival at the store to their sales location without any additional storage inside the store. Another priority has been to review all sales packaging, to increase the amount of goods on pallets, and to maximize the ready to sell packaging coming into the store that requires minimum re-merchandising.

The use of technology and IT to improve the conditions of the store has increased substantially in importance during the last few years. It is difficult to believe that only 10 years ago, we didn't have Facebook, YouTube, the iPod, the iPhone, and home broadband. The digital revolution is no doubt a blessing for improving sales and operational processes in the store, but it is also a formidable competition for the customer's wallet. We see declining spending on home furnishings in favor of electronics and telecommunication.

Maybe the most important example of improving the conditions of the store is the use of the Web to prepare store visits. In only around 10 years, visits to the Ikea website have increased from virtually zero to 500 million per year. IT and digital media will become more and more important to the store experience when it comes to improving services (i.e., self-serve checkouts, product price checks, loyalty cards, customer credits), operations (i.e., pricing, tracking stock movements), and sales (i.e., showing more solutions and showing how to apply the products). New technology will help improve work processes for the employees, but, even more important, it can help integrate the customer more into the sales process.

Motivating the Customer

A second strategy is to integrate the customer even more into the sales process. I think that when customers feel that they are in charge of an activity, they often perceive it as better service even if it means more work for them. An Ikea example is the introduction of the already mentioned self-serve checkouts, a technique that can be introduced also for product returns.

On the Ikea website, customers can look for products and ideas but can also download kitchen planning systems, allowing them to plan kitchen designs themselves and digitally coordinate final adjustments and payment. This solution is also being introduced for other areas of the range. In the future, perhaps customers will also be able to do all steps in the sales process themselves. This development will be a key driver to productivity improvements in the years to come.

Focus on the People

The third strategy involves the people management of the store. Seventy-five percent of Ikea employees work in the stores. The most important task of the store is to attract, develop, and retain good people. This is a challenging task in a retail environment. In my opinion, some key factors in creating conditions to successfully develop a store are to contain staff fluctuation to around 20 percent per year; to have no less than 40 to 50 percent full-time employees; and to retain store management, ideally for five years but no less than three years. This stability and continuity is necessary to avoid being stuck in daily challenges and to avoid just coping with the day-to-day business rather than developing it. Strong leadership, focus on competence development, and good staff planning are key to good people management.

Benchmarking

The fourth strategy is benchmarking to drive store performance. In the nineties, Ikea started a commercial review process where the standards of all areas of the store were defined and then the most experienced people were used to make reviews of the stores on a regular basis. The process was led from the Ikea Group level, but over time, more and more of the work was delegated to each country organization. The review process started as a control activity, but over time it matured and is today seen more as a training and learning activity.

In 2006, another system was put in place, wherein all Ikea stores and countries were measured and compared on different key performance indices (KPI). Everything from sales, productivity, and direct deliver shares to different service measurements was compared—in total around 20 different KPIs. Interestingly, for most KPIs, the difference between the best and the worst performing stores was more than 100 percent. So with the same range, the same concept stores, the same working methods and IT systems, and the same training programs, it is still possible to have large differences between stores. The company was putting many resources into different new development projects, but at the same time it was evident that if Ikea could just move all stores up to the level of the best 25 percent of stores for each KPI, the potential to improve the results was significant. These results could be achieved practically without any new development. It was just a matter of copying what the best stores were already doing.

These two examples illustrate the challenge of managing both innovation and execution. Ikea is, perhaps, better at innovation than it is at execution. The challenge is to maintain this strength but at the same time to become better at execution. Doing so calls for more centralization, standardization, discipline, and control—all of which, in many respects, can be seen as the very antidote of an innovative business environment. Becoming both innovative and execution oriented at the same time is no easy challenge. Freedom versus control. Change versus standardization. Decentralization versus centralization. Innovation versus execution. Managing these contradictions is a big challenge. Many have failed, ending up with only the disadvantages of the big company, such as bureaucracy and complacency. Some have mastered the advantages of being big, such as economies of scale and efficiency, but have lost personality and a small company feel.

Ikea is still in this transformation phase and needs to make sure that it can achieve both innovation and execution while remaining a company with a heart and soul.

To sum up, achieving high store standards and productivity calls for a strategy of:

- Setting the right conditions for the store
- Integrating the customer even more into the sale process
- Strong people management
- Benchmarking to improve store standards and operations

CHAPTER 9

Effective Communication

C ommunication or marketing has always been one of the most frustrating disciplines for me. When listening to endless complicated presentations on market segmentation, brand advertising, and "customer insights," I feel tempted to go back and apply the Dilbert principle of marketing: "All you need to know is that if you lower the price, you can sell more units." And very often it is as simple as that.

The Media Mix

In order of importance, the Ikea media mix consists of:

* Stores
* The Web
* The Catalog
* The Ikea Family club
* Brochures
* Television and print advertising

Annually, there are more than 600 million visitors to the stores and 500 million visits to the website. Of course, this is where most of the marketing money needs to be invested.

The Stores

The importance of the stores is obvious, and it has not been lost on Ikea. Over the years, the company has developed the store concept and improved various merchandising techniques.

The steered customer flow is one important principle of the store. Many customers complain about having to walk long distances to get to the checkouts. Many tests have been conducted to determine if the more traditional free-flow system used by most retailers would work better, but so far the conclusion has always been in favor of a steered customer flow.

Providing a full overview of the product range is another important principle of the store. We know that most customers want help with combining products to get the best solutions for their home. The Ikea answer to that need has been the ready-made room sets in the showroom combined with big areas where the full range is displayed. Many customers talk about how impossible it is to leave the store without buying something. An attractive product range and good prices are, of course, the most important reasons for this. But another significant factor is the many merchandising techniques the company uses, where every product has its specific place and job to do in promoting low prices, design, quality, product choice, etc. The company tests many new solutions constantly, and they are gradually introduced into the stores when proven successful. To the regular visitor, many of these changes are probably hardly recognizable. This model is evolutionary rather than revolutionary. Even so, it is amazing how many of the old truths have stood the test of time.

Ikea is often asked when it will develop city center concepts. Personally, I do not believe in this. The very power and unique point of difference with the Ikea concept is the fact that everything for the home is available in one place. Any city center concept would compromise this, since due to higher property prices and lack of available facilities, city center stores would necessarily be smaller. I prefer big stores outside city centers in combination with Web-based sales for inner-city people.

The Power of the Web

The Ikea website has increased enormously in importance in the past 10 years and has big potential for the future both in showing and selling an extended range and in preparing customers for the store visit. In addition, the Ikea catalog has been an icon in the media mix for many years. From the very beginning, the mass distribution of the Ikea catalog to all households in the catchment area of the store was an important part of the Ikea identity.

However, in the past few years, the catalog has come under pressure. It is no longer unique; many other companies distribute big catalogs in many markets. Many new local store markets and big cities with very big populations make it financially impossible to mass distribute the company's catalog to all households. In many countries, apartment blocs are locked, preventing access to distributors. As well, more and more people have put "No thank you to advertising" on their mailboxes.

In my opinion, the company could improve developing the catalogs so that they feel different and more exciting year after year. The catalog still has an important role to play in the Ikea media mix, but there is a need to change the distribution model. More targeted distribution through the Ikea Family club on the one hand, plus free distribution to the many households via pickup in the store, on the other hand, would be my preferred distribution model.

The Difficulties of Centralization

Ikea communication is centrally steered by the company. Both the content (range and price steering) and the layout of the stores, website, catalog, Ikea Family club, and brochures are prepared centrally to maximize the commercial impact of the range priorities. The part that is left to local adaptation is television and print advertising. Not surprisingly, this is also the part that is least consistent in quality.

During my 26 years in the company, I can think of two, maybe three periods when Ikea had really good TV and print advertising in a local market, which contributed to lifting the brand position of the company. I have seen many more examples where campaigns have been unfavorable to the brand. Ad campaigns work on those rare occasions when an excellent marketing manager meets an excellent advertising agency. I prefer solid price or product communication in cost efficient media such as the store, the Web, and the Family club, which is Web-based. This approach may not contribute to big movements in the perception of the brand, but it supports the daily bread and butter of marketing, bringing visitors to the store. The Dilbert principle in action, if you like.

Let me close this chapter with a couple of words about the Ikea restaurants. The restaurants have grown to a business of $1.5 billion (€1 billion) in sales. However, at Ikea, the restaurants are viewed as part of the communication mix rather than as a profit center. This is one of the secrets to the very low prices in the restaurants and food shops. The restaurants are there to sell more home furnishings by encouraging people to remain in the store for a longer time. The Ikea Food Service (IFS) supports the price image with the low prices, and it helps keep the customers in the store longer. People with full stomachs are inclined to stay longer at the store.

CHAPTER 10

Working as *One* Company

Big global retail companies such as Ikea face two important questions and potential contradictions when establishing the best ways of organizational structure and day-to-day operations. One is how to combine strong specialist functions within "one" company view and approach. In other words, they must grapple with how to combine a functional and a process-oriented organization. To reiterate an earlier point, differentiation through controlling the whole value chain is key to success. This will only be achieved, though, if the company can make it work in an efficient and integrated way. The answer to that challenge is process orientation.

The second question for companies is how to combine an entrepreneurial spirit with room for individual initiatives in order to integrate speedy decisions with an efficient, streamlined organization where scale advantages can be achieved through coordination, common procedures, and structure.

The Power of Integration

To the outside world, Ikea has probably always come across as a very well-coordinated organization. This is partly true. There are some very important factors that have helped keep the company together: a strong vision, the business idea, company values, a common store concept, a common product range, and a common distribution and buying organization. All these things have been very important success factors since the early days of the company. Still, my biggest concern when I became CEO in 1999 was that we did not work very well together.

There were several reasons for this. First, it was part of the company's heritage and not uncommon in many young organizations. The entrepreneurial spirit had guided Ikea from the start. With little coordination and a small overhead structure, the company was moving fast without spending time thinking about coordination and common ways of working. Coordination, in fact, was considered a sign of bureaucracy.

The people who were attracted to the company wanted freedom to do things their own way, and these strong personalities built their own "kingdoms" with highly motivated employees. These people, in turn, had the freedom to try out new things and develop the business pretty much any way they wanted. In my former roles at the company, I had thoroughly enjoyed this freedom.

At no time during my prior 16 years in the company had we possessed a common overall Ikea Group plan for the company. There were different initiatives from time to time, yes, of course, but only short lived, limited plans. There were no common global objectives and strategies linking the very broad vision and business idea with the many local plans existing in the different units of the company. Consequently, the different organizations had developed their own agendas trying to optimize their own areas of responsibility. Every retail market worked independently; as well, the buying organization, the distribution organization, and the range development organization each had separate objectives. Each tried to convince the other parts of the organization to do things their way.

The negative consequences of this approach became more apparent as Ikea grew larger. The level of trust deteriorated between retail, range, distribution, and buying. The retail countries' central organizations were growing fast, trying to do everything themselves.

Because the supply chain did not work well, the company did not come to terms with product availability problems, overstock, and quality issues. As a result, overhead costs were rising faster than sales growth. It seemed as though we were uncomfortable with the thought of more coordination and common procedures as a solution because this might have meant leaving our comfortable, entrepreneurial way of working. We didn't see the solution clearly, and at the same time we were afraid that this would change the company into something we didn't want.

For me, this was the biggest challenge of my new job. We needed to transform Ikea so that it could continue to grow and prosper. This transformation would mean some big changes in our ways of working.

The first step was to create a common plan—"Ten Jobs in Ten Years." This 10-year direction would be the foundation upon which to bring the organization together with a common agenda. One of the 10 tasks in this plan was labeled "To be One Ikea." Here is a quote from the actual plan:

> Ikea is a company with many disciplines and many markets. We must always remember that Ikea's competitive edge comes when all the disciplines work together selflessly and take the Ikea perspective. We want managers and co-workers who understand all aspects of Ikea's operations; people who can think about their function, but are able to think like Ikea owners too. When managers and co-workers are genuinely interested in sharing and accepting ideas from each other, then we will be using the competence and resources of the whole company. We must break down all barriers, between functions and markets, and build an open and trustful working climate, and that way, act as One Ikea.

Two Main Initiatives

We approached this big question with two principle initiatives. The company needed to change its thinking from a functional method to a process-oriented way of working. Main processes and subprocesses had to be defined, and then managers had to align working methods and the IT system to these processes. That way we hoped to crack the problem of the main functions—retail, range, distribution, and buying—not working well together.

The second initiative involved aligning the work between all the different retail markets. This initiative was called "better retailing."

The Process Orientation Initiative

Professor Russel Ackoff is one of the pioneers of system thinking and management science. I think this quotation very well illustrates the merits of looking at work as processes rather than functions:

> If you put all cars of this world in one room and then you pick out the best parts from the best cars, that is, you take the best engine among all the cars, the best steering wheel, the best exhaust pipe, etc., and at the end, you would have all the different parts necessary to build a car but coming from many different car models and brands. The question is, if you put them together would you have the best car? Or rather would you have a functioning car at all? Probably not. The result does not come from how well the parts work in isolation. The success comes from their ability to work together. That is what makes the best car.

In 1999, Ikea was a car that worked, but barely. The main problem was the inability to work together and through that produce the best results. The Ikea business is now structured along three core processes and some support processes. The core processes are supplying, creating the offer, and communicating and selling. The support processes are finance, human resources, and management planning.

The core processes. The most important core process that we needed to establish was the supply process. In the previous chapter, I described how the company did this. This was also the process through which the fastest change and results were achieved with a new organization and new management. The "creating the offer" process also worked fairly well, partly because it involved fewer people and less system change requirements. The "communication and selling" process has been the most difficult to improve. This required extensive cooperation between the functional organizations range development and retail. A long history of problems and lack of trust between these organizations did not help, and it was a struggle to find common views and common solutions. Step by step, however, the company aligned important subprocesses such as pricing, phasing in and out of products, the commercial agenda, marketing, store planning, range launches, and sales steering.

The range development organization or, in Ikea lingo, IoS (Ikea of Sweden), is the hub of the company. Range creation is the starting point of everything. IoS then connects with the supply organization to plan production capacities. As well, IoS connects with retail to plan strategic pricing, the commercial agenda, and the selling and communication activities to promote sales. When these activities work in harmony based on a common agenda and common objectives, Ikea is unbeatable.

Better Retailing Initiative

The best way to describe this initiative is to quote from the "better retailing" document used to launch it.

- "Looking back how we have been running our retail operations within Ikea over the years, the strategy has been to build up independent country units. Development and coordinating resources at Group level have been very slim and each country has been responsible for building up the resources it takes to develop and run its operation. Although this has been a successful formula over the years there are some important missed opportunities in this way of working, considering that Ikea is a big, global company with a common range and a common concept."
- "The bargaining power derived through scale of operations making it possible to buy big quantities and thus getting better prices than other smaller companies."

- "The resources (financial and competence) that when coordinated make it possible to develop and invest in commercial and operational systems and methods on a scale that give us major improvements compared to smaller companies."
- "The possibility to pool resources and through that derive scale of economies in our operations."
- "The possibility to access ideas and competence from many different places and transfer these from one part of the organization to another."
- "Through our way of working over the years we have not made sufficient use of these advantages. To the extent it has happened it has been more the result of independent initiatives than a conscious overall strategy. Independence and competition between retail units had been the driving force rather than cooperation."
- "Looking at how we have chosen to operate within each country unit I feel there has been a shift over the years from more independent stores to more centrally steered operations with bigger overhead organizations at Service Office (the country central organization). As a consequence we have lost some of that important entrepreneurial spirit where business opportunities are acted upon quickly and local initiatives are encouraged. The advantage of a small business has been lost. With this way of working we have seen many good improvements but we have also seen increasing overhead costs, less flexibility and less initiatives to adapt and react to changes in sales and customer demands—less ownership in the stores."
- "In short, we have not sufficiently used the advantages of big organizations and we have lost some of the advantages of small companies that we used to have."
- "A vision for the future!"
- "In the future we want to have the cake and eat it too! We want to explore the advantages of the big global Ikea but also get the advantage of the small entrepreneurial company."
- "We want to centralize and decentralize, we want to integrate and differentiate, both at the same time. We want very motivated, experienced and independent retailers in our stores. We

want a lean, effective, highly competent supportive Service Office organization with a passion to give the best possible service to the stores. We want a small, highly competent global retail organization that supports cooperation, development, transfer of ideas and the effective use of our global advantages. We want a much closer and better cooperation between stores, Service Office, Ikea of Sweden, Distribution, Trading and Inter Ikea Systems."

"One Ikea"

The central country organizations (service offices) had increased in size by 50 percent between 1998 and 2001, to a total of 1,500 people. One reason, of course, was that the number of stores had increased, but, more important and more worrying, was that the countries were doing more and more of their own development. The lack of quality work from the range and supply organizations meant the service offices needed more resources to correct or adapt information and other input (this was before the process orientation initiative had taken hold), and there was a tendency to centralize tasks and detail-steer the stores from the country level.

Having our cake and eating it too meant two things. We had to take advantage of being big with more global coordination, but, at the same time, we needed to return to the time when stores had a bigger mandate to run their own operations. The ones losing out in this scenario were the central country organizations, and these were the very people who had to make much of the change.

What were some of the things that should be coordinated globally? Within human resources, there were a number of opportunities. Because all countries had different HR systems and working methods, by harmonizing these, Ikea could procure common HR administration systems, recruitment systems, and so forth. Additionally, it could introduce shared service centers. Since the entire company had the same range and store concept, there was no need to spend time in each country to develop training programs anymore. Instead, Ikea created a retail training college together with the franchiser Inter Ikea Systems for all markets to use. The country office focused on implementing programs rather than developing them. This way development costs could be reduced, and more people could be trained.

In the area of our restaurants, every store did its own procurement. The potential for global sourcing was very great regarding food as well as restaurant equipment. Also, in the area of finance, there was the potential for common working methods and systems as well as shared services.

In common procurement areas such as media, store equipment, catalogs, construction, office supply, electricity, and IT, a global procurement organization was created for everything that was not within the Ikea range.

There was also potential for further standardizing store planning for rebuilds and new stores, including layout and division and planning of each department, down to the design of common room sets in the stores. This was not only a cost-saving exercise but also helped in the development of the communicating and selling process so that the company could achieve a stronger coordination in the whole pipeline of the commercial priorities.

The company's leadership decided that all managers down to shopkeeper level in the stores should learn to speak English. Doing this reduced the need to translate all information coming from the range and supply functions to the stores. As a consequence, it was possible to speed up communication substantially and save costs.

Better Information

With the parallel initiative of process orientation, the company's intent was to improve the quality of information coming to the stores from various parts in the organization so that the country service offices could reduce time spent on adapting or correcting this input. Major retail development projects could still be initiated at a country level, but if they qualified as global solutions, the global retail function would manage them.

More marketing communication was coordinated globally and shared among countries, including catalogs, brochures, Internet sites, and the Ikea Family club concept.

The company also wanted to give more freedom to the stores. For instance, we asked the stores to take charge of the analysis of local competition and their markets, much of which had been done by the central service office. They were also asked to create their own marketing plans. Local store boards were introduced as a way to clarify responsibility. A store participation model was launched wherein a store manager could take on the role as owner of his or her store.

All these initiatives meant that more resources were needed at a global level. My fear was that we would not see a corresponding reduction of resources in the central country organizations unless some drastic actions were taken. So we communicated that our ambition now was to reduce the service offices by 50 percent. I didn't have a clue if 50 percent was the right number, but I was willing to take the chance. Even if we slimmed the organizations too much in some places, overall this was necessary to kick-start the change into action.

The efficiency improvement was measured as a ratio of service office employees per store. This felt more fair, given that at the same time as this change happened, many new stores were also opened. Between 2001 and 2006, the ratio of service office employees per store was reduced by 30 percent and, excluding new start-up markets, the ratio was closer to 40 percent. Some markets actually managed to reduce the number by 50 percent even in absolute terms. In the same time, 2001 to 2006, global units increased by a total of 50 people. In that period, in percentage of sales, the global functions cost ratio decreased from 0.24 percent to 0.20 percent. However, by 2008, the cost ratio for global function had risen to 0.33 percent.

In total, global staff functions, including finance, HR, marketing, sales, restaurants, property, legal, and so forth had around 260 people in 2008. The company had around 125,000 employees and sales revenues of $29 billion (€20 billion). The global overhead functions still felt at a reasonable level.

Some Reflections

What are the pros and cons of such a transformation? In my opinion, it is not a question of having a process-oriented or a functional organization, nor is it a question of having a centralized or a decentralized organization. *It is both.* You need functions like buying and range development with strong specialists, but you also need these people to have an attitude and willingness to cooperate across functions and work for the benefit of the company as a whole, not just for the benefit of their function or area of responsibility. In reality, many managers and specialists are not equipped for that. Ikea had many strong managers who thrived only when they could totally control their own areas with little or no cooperation with others. Sometimes the company found suitable tasks for these people.

One example was the start-up in Russia, during which a group of managers was mandated to focus only on that task. This created a lot of frustration in other parts of the organization, but for that specific task in that challenging environment, they were best suited to prevail. But in most cases, the ability to cooperate is an important management attribute. I sometimes excluded strong performers from further promotion because I was not comfortable with their ability to cooperate and work for the benefit of the totality.

It is also necessary to have both a central and local focus. Centralized or global functions should exist, where it makes sense to benefit from being a big company. If you are not willing to accept the benefits of this, I would argue that it is probably better to break up the company. Being big makes sense only if there are substantial advantages to be derived from it.

Local responsibility is always important. In the retail world, store management has an enormous impact on performance. The difference between a good and a bad store manager can mean a difference in store profitability of 100 percent or more. Good people will stay motivated in the stores if they feel that they are fully in charge of their operations.

The central country organizations are there primarily to bridge the size of the organization. The main task is to convey information to the stores from other parts of the organization: best practices, new development projects, etc. In the ideal world, this could come directly from the source to each store, packaged in an easy-to-use way.

A second task for the central country organization is to build new stores. The third task should be to contribute to global development. If possible, global development should happen close to the market, not in a corporate office. It is important to keep a close eye on the size of these central organizations because they have a tendency to grow.

A key question, of course, is if this change is making Ikea more bureaucratic. If you equate bureaucracy with being slow in change and slow in making decisions, being too complex, having unnecessary costs not adding value, and not seeing the effects of different initiatives, I would say no. Not if the alternative is the old model where the functions did not cooperate well and all retail markets worked more or less in isolation. If the financial results are any indication, the initiative has been a resounding success. Ikea has seen sales growth triple between 2000 and 2009; total costs as well as relative overhead costs have been reduced; and there has been some strong profit development. I don't think that would have been possible had Ikea continued with the old format.

This new way of working can be further improved, and that work will probably take another few years to fine-tune and develop to a next level. But I am certain that it is the right direction if Ikea wants to continue to grow as one company.

Negative Effects

Today there is much more pressure within the company to perform. There is a higher degree of professionalism. There is more need of structure, and for many employees, there is less time and fewer opportunities to try out new solutions. Is this unavoidable? I think increasing size does create more distance, adds to complexity, and increases the consequences of mistakes and wrong decisions.

If you want to grow as one company, some of these negative effects are unavoidable, and you have to accept them. However, I have always said that I believe that the biggest threat to Ikea is Ikea itself. Some worry that some new technological innovation will come along and change the game of home furnishing retailing in a way that would jeopardize Ikea. However, I think this is unlikely. Competitors so far have shown little sign of innovation, and people will, I assume, need home furnishings in the future. No, the big threat is from within. Even if important steps are taken to structure the business to cope with increasing size, as described in this chapter, increasing complexity and size, complacency, and the gradual decline of the values and vision when the founder is gone are all likely to have a negative impact on the rate of innovation, loyalty, and motivation among employees in coming years. It may sound strange, but a continuation of today's successful growth may be sowing the seeds for future decline. It will certainly be a big challenge for future owner generations and managers to counter this development.

Daring to be different may be the only way for Ikea to renew itself. As I have stated several times, I believe the entrepreneurial way to do business is the most successful one. At some point, any company might become too big to be able to work in that way and start on the path of decline. Maybe an alternative is to break up the company and start anew in smaller independent units with new, dedicated, capable owners in charge. I don't personally know of any company that has chosen to do that from such a position of strength as that occupied by Ikea today. But who knows? Ikea has always done things differently. Maybe it is time to do that again.

CHAPTER 11

Staying on Track

All business models are internally challenged from time to time. This is justifiable, if the offer is no longer in demand or it has lost its unique point of difference and competitive advantages for reasons outside company control. But what happens when the business concept is challenged because of internal mistakes, even if the model itself is sound? This often happens when a company is under pressure from competition or in an economic downturn with low general demand in the market. With falling sales and increasing costs, the company is looking for easy wins. This could mean adapting the products on offer to be more mainstream or increasing prices to offset higher costs. I have seen this happen a few times at Ikea. You may get some short-term gains in your profit and loss statement, but you will invariably lose your unique identity and consequently lose your point of difference.

One example of this is Ikea's development in the late eighties and early nineties. In 1983, the organization's international expansion changed focus. Germany entered a consolidation phase, and it would take 10 years until the next German store opening. The following important new markets were France (1984), the United States (1985), the UK (1988), and Italy (1989). The expansion strategy was to go wide but thin—open a few stores in a market and then move on to the next. I never understood the eagerness to quickly move on to new markets instead of growing the markets that had just opened. Maybe there was a belief that markets were saturated already with a few stores because Ikea represented something different that only a small part of the population would be attracted to. Maybe it was simply the spirit and enthusiasm of the company at the time.

Nevertheless, the company was stretching itself thin. Opening in many new markets in a short time quickly increased the cost level. The United States and Eastern European markets didn't respond as well as previous new markets, and Ikea started losing money in these countries. The company compensated for this by increasing the sales prices to maintain the gross margin, but, as a consequence, price competitiveness deteriorated. Sales growth in comparable units slowed down. Many markets were screaming for a more locally adapted range to boost sales quickly. Accomodating these demands, the range size was increasing fast. As a consequence, volume advantages in the buying were decreasing, and Ikea lost control of the supply chain. Buying prices increased, product quality problems became more frequent, poor product availability in the stores became an increasing problem, and, with a more locally adapted range, the unique range identity risked getting blurred. A well-intentioned cost reduction project was started, but some of the unwanted effects of this were a reduction in service quality to customers, with long waiting times in the checkouts, too few parking spaces, and little investment in the existing stores.

Navigating a Period of Drift

Ikea was reacting to problems with solutions that took the company further and further away from the successful formula built up over many years. During the late eighties and beginning of the nineties, sales prices were increasing by some 3 percent every year, and the cost level peaked in 1992.

Internally, the relationship and trust level between the main parts of the organization (supply, range, and retail markets) were deteriorating. Everyone blamed each other, and there was no over-all, common, forward-looking agenda.

The size of the company also began to pose a problem, as the working methods and systems were still those of a small company. There was no clear idea how to transform into the big company Ikea was becoming. There was a reluctance to behave like and become a big company. The company was searching for the right organization structure; two big reorganizations in four years took a lot of energy and focus away from the business. Ikea was drifting, not knowing where to go next.

This was not a good period for Ikea. I think what triggered this chain of events was the combination of opening too many new markets too quickly; not realizing that moving outside western Europe meant more than just copying what had been done before; a severe slowdown in the economy; the lack of an overall direction for the company; and confusion around the transformation from a small to a big company. This put pressure on sales and profitability, and Ikea didn't have an answer to the problem.

However, the crisis forced some change, and in 1995 the company began to return to some of the fundamentals of Ikea's success criteria. The product range strategy was sharpened, reducing the range size and improving its identity. The leadership team created a clear and successful purchasing strategy built on reducing the supplier base and moving production to low cost countries. Sales prices were reduced again, and an investment program in the existing stores began. Between 1995 and 1998, Ikea opened in only two new markets (Finland and Spain), which was few compared with previous years. The economy was turning, and the company started to see a positive development in almost all markets.

What I and the rest of the leadership team learned from this experience was that Ikea's basic concept is successful when you stick to it:

- Aggressive pricing with big price distance to competitors
- Unique range identity with limited depth
- Focus on low purchase prices through a production adapted range

- Continued investments in stores, prices, quality, and people also when the economy is getting tough

A strong economy combined with some of these positive changes paid off, and during the period 1995–1998, Ikea was experiencing strong sales growth and good profitability. In short, almost every company experiences a period of drift over time—it's how you handle it that counts.

PART 3

Market Leadership and a Balanced Market Portfolio

n this section, I will discuss some examples from the Ikea global expansion over the past 10 years, focusing on a few important markets. This will illustrate some of the strategic questions and challenges global companies are facing. Then I will draw some conclusions regarding challenges and opportunities the retail sector (and probably other sectors too) needs to consider in order to prosper in a global environment.

Planning for the Future

The 25-year expansion period from 1973 to 1998 had been something of a roller coaster with many ups and downs. But by 1998, sales had grown from $5.7 million (€40 million) to $9.1 billion (€6.3 billion) and stores from 7 to 120. Ikea was ready for the next phase.

As always, Ikea had a number of challenges and opportunities. There was confusion about how to adapt the ways of working and the systems to the size and growth of the company. Overhead organizations continued to grow. The company was becoming increasingly bureaucratic. It needed a plan for how to become successful in the United States and Eastern Europe. We were just on the verge of entering Russia and China, two new and very different markets. Product availability and service in stores still was a big concern. There had been some bad publicity around environmental and social issues (formaldehyde in the products and child labor at suppliers in Pakistan), but there was no comprehensive plan in place for dealing with this.

A new direction for the company was needed, and in 1999, my first priority as CEO was to put this in place. I felt this was urgently needed. We were a disjointed organization. Lots of short-term actions and local plans meant lack of stability, uncertainty about direction, suboptimization of the parts, and a lack of overall leadership. The process of developing this undertaking was not exactly a schoolbook example of planning in the sense that it was a very top-down approach. The company needed a few months to establish the new management team, and there simply wasn't time to wait and involve them in the process.

This approach was met with some skepticism. Not only was it a change to have a common Ikea Group direction—this direction was developed without broader involvement of the organization. Finally and not least, it had a 10-year perspective!

"What plan can survive and be relevant for 10 years?" some within the company asked.

The Reasons behind the 10-Year Plan

This was admittedly a bit unusual, but there were some good reasons for taking this approach. Ikea was in a situation where stability and confidence about where the company was heading were crucial. There was also a need to trigger employees' imaginations to see the great opportunities for the future. A three- or five-year plan was too short to do that job. Anchoring a plan, as well as seeing the effects of it in an organization the size of Ikea, would take some time.

I often feel that planning periods are so short that by the time a plan is finalized, organizations start on a new planning process. There must be enough time to do the job. Also, shorter plans tend to be very operational and deal more with incremental improvements in today's agenda rather than dealing with major shifts.

The direction for Ikea was called "Ten Jobs in Ten Years (10/10)." The idea was that it should marry the long-term vision of the company—"to create a better everyday life for the many"—with the short-term operational plans in the different subdivisions of the company.

What was the direction of this 10-year plan? Let's go directly to the source with some quotes from the goal description.

Out Receipt

Mill Bethany Branch Library
17-7323
//www.wccls.org

day, October 15, 2015 7:02:45 PM

33614052261475
: The everything store : Jeff Bezos and the
of Amazon
ial: Books
11/05/2015

33614047628747
: The IKEA edge : building global growth an
ial good at the world's most iconic home st

ial: Books
11/05/2015

items: 2

cement Levy for Countywide Library Services
re 34-235
ore information:
d the November 3rd Voters Pamphlet
a local librarian about Measure 34-235
on to wccls.org/levy
503-846-3222

Ikea must grow. Our vision is to improve the everyday lives of the majority of people, and so far we have only improved the everyday lives of some. We must grow to reach our vision, to give ourselves new opportunities and to keep ahead of the competition in a changing competitive environment. So far growth has come from going "wide but thin." We have stores in twenty-nine countries but with limited market share in most markets. Now we enter a new phase where the focus will be to go "deep" and concentrate on our existing markets. We will strengthen the relationship with our customers and make sure we are their preferred choice. We shall be the leading home furnishing company in the markets in which we operate. Our goal will be to reach a substantial share in all our present European and North American markets by 2010, and take the step and really become accessible and accepted by the majority of people—to implement our vision. We shall focus on continued strong volume growth, 10 percent per year for 10 years (group average in existing units). In Asia-Pacific, the big challenge will be to gain a strong foothold in the countries we have already chosen to enter (China, Australia, Japan) and to get to a point of profitability. This will also be the ambition for our new important market, Russia. To reach our goal, we will need to find ways to open more than 100 new stores and triple group sales, exceeding 200BSEK by 2010.

This statement represented a dramatic change from what the company had been doing up to that point.

- This was a growth strategy as opposed to the cost-reduction strategy of the early nineties.
- This was a strategy based on growth in existing markets as opposed to prioritizing the opening of new markets.
- This was a strategy with more store openings than ever before.
- This was a strategy for growth and profitability in the non-European markets.

* This was an aggressive strategy to grow in comparable units with 10 percent per year for 10 years. (Ikea had grown with an average of 6 percent during the nineties.)

Setting Out the Business Strategy

Let me continue with another quote from the goal description:

> Our business idea is to offer a wide range of well-designed, functional home furnishing products at prices so low that as many people as possible will be able to afford them. Say we were to hold our sales prices level for the next ten years. This might sound impressive! But we live in a changing world, with next to zero inflation in most markets and with increased global competition that is developing the same strengths as we have. In this context, level prices are not good enough. In order to reach our vision, live up to our business idea, reach our volume targets and compete successfully, our goal will be to reduce our sales prices to at least 20 percent below today's level by 2010 on group level.

Again, this was a major shift compared to the company's strategy up to this point, one where price increases had been the norm for many years.

Why make the change? First of all, we were impelled by the changing character of the competition. For many years, the competition had been very fragmented and local in nature. However, many of the very big retail companies were shifting strategy. From being local, they were looking to a global expansion, not least in the emerging markets like China, Russia, and Eastern Europe.

They were also broadening their product range, moving away from food or traditional DIY products toward more home furnishing. These were big companies with much more muscle than Ikea's traditional competitors. They had both financial resources and operational retailing competence on par with Ikea. One way to dissuade them from entering into the home furnishing arena was to aggressively reduce prices and increase the company's presence with more stores in all local markets in the countries where Ikea was operating. Market leadership in each market was the objective.

Another reason for the shift in strategy was cost efficiency. Growing sales in existing stores is the most cost-efficient way to grow the company. Second to that is to build new stores in existing markets. The most expensive option is to open in new markets. Opening many new markets very quickly in the seventies, eighties, and nineties had had some negative consequences, as earlier described. Now this could be turned into an advantage, and Ikea could reap a harvest from these earlier investments. A big part of the cost base being fixed also meant that strong growth in existing units would immediately give a strong leverage in operating profits.

A third reason for the plan's change in strategy was motivation. Ikea thrives on growth. Its history is all about growth. And I believe opening new stores is the engine of most retailing. Nothing motivates employees more than being part of building a new store. The fact that the 10/10 plan was telling the organization that growth in the existing markets was a priority was a great motivator for many employees and managers.

Finally, another reason was more philosophical. The Ikea company vision is to create a better everyday life for the majority of people. If we truly mean that Ikea will be accessible to the majority of people, prices must be reduced so that everyone can afford the products, even those living in emerging markets. The company must also be present with substantially more stores in enough areas to serve the majority of people.

Profitability Goals

Here's another quote from the goal formulation, to give you a more complete idea:

> Profit is important to us because it allows us to move towards our vision of improving the everyday lives of the many people. Profit is not an end for us but a means. Profit must always be

achieved through low costs. A low price company must also be a low cost company. Cost-consciousness must be a part of every priority. Having said that, our vision is a long-term vision, and it can only be achieved with strong profitability on a long-term basis. This means we must be prepared to accept a lower level of profit, in the short term, if this puts us in a stronger long-term position. So when the economy slows down, we will continue to invest in our concept, sticking to the investment programs in our stores, sticking to our training programs and our pricing targets. This will give us long-term profitability as well as better stability and consistency in our actions, which will benefit our co-workers, our customers, our suppliers and our owners.

What was the thinking behind this statement? Ikea is a foundation and has decided to be self-reliant in financing its growth. With the growth ambitions for the 10-year period, this meant a substantial profit level was needed to be able to finance an increasing number of stores, warehouses, and factories. The ambition was to never go below 10 percent operating profit level (percent of sales), in any of these 10 years.

Based on the bad experience of the economic downturn in the nineties, the idea was to look at the next downturn in another way. Many companies have a short-sighted way of handling changes in the economy. When writing the 10/10 plan, we were in the middle of the IT boom of the late nineties. So we did some scenario planning to establish what the consequences would be if, in the next downturn, Ikea lost 5 percent, 10 percent, or more in sales. Based on these scenarios, we presented alternatives to the board and asked for their support of a strategy in which Ikea chose to accelerate its investments instead of cutting costs when the economy was slowing down the next time.

Doing so, we reasoned, the company could come out of the next downturn with all sails set and substantially increase its distance from the competition. This approach was approved by the board in December 1999. Consequently, when the downturn came in 2001,

Ikea was reducing sales prices and increasing investments in both existing and new stores.

Again, the company did things differently from others in the industry. I think it is easier to get the commitment for a strategy like this in a privately held company because you need to accept the possibility of lower profits in the short term to get a medium-term upside. It is more difficult to gain acceptance of a risk like this with uncertain returns, I believe, in a listed company.

Did Ikea reach the financial goals in the 10-year plan? Sales tripled from $10.9 billion (€7.6 billion) in 1999 to $30.9 billion (€21.5 billion) in 2009. Sales prices and purchase prices were both reduced by 20 percent, and the profit levels were well above 10 percent of sales in all 10 years. All was in line with the plan.

The one disappointment was that the cost level did not decrease as much as planned. We'd needed productivity gains of 10 percent per year or more, and we managed only around a 4 to 6 percent productivity improvement per year on average. Better than planned margins compensated for this, and thus the profit level was in line with the plan. Nevertheless, a low price company must be a low cost company.

CHAPTER 12

The Market Strategy

An important question for any global retailer to explore is which markets to operate in. Developing a strategy for figuring this out involves a number of tasks and issues:

1. Establishing a well-balanced portfolio of markets with short-term, mid-term, and long-term growth and profitability potential
2. Evaluating the potential power of the offer in different markets—the potential to become one of the leading companies in its category
3. Balancing risk versus potential
4. Evaluating the importance of trade barriers
5. Looking at the potential limitations of the resources and values of the organization
6. Evaluating the importance of speed versus a more measured, gradual growth
7. Reflecting on potential needs to adapt the business model
8. Finding out how to become a valued contributor in the society of new markets

Approaching Market Strategy

How did Ikea approach these questions? In 1999, Europe contributed around 80 percent of Ikea's sales, the United States 17 percent, and Asia-Pacific 3 percent. Europe was the solid profitable home base. The United States was struggling, and Russia and Asia-Pacific were both in their initial stages as future growth markets.

An aggressive expansion strategy in the existing markets became one important part of the Ikea 10/10 plan. The company wanted to consolidate Europe and firmly position Ikea as the market leader in each European market. The plan also projected fixing the United States and building a successful business in the new markets of Asia-Pacific and Russia—the markets of the future. In the beginning of the planning period (1999), the company was down to only five new store openings per year, representing 3 percent of all stores. At the end of the period, the pace had increased to around 20 new stores per year, or 9 percent of all stores. In total over the 10-year period 2000–2009, Ikea opened 150 stores, more than the 130 stores that had been opened in the previous 55 years. Of those new stores, approximately 110 were opened in Europe (including Russia), 25 in North America, and 15 in Asia.

The stores also got bigger. In 2009, an average new store was around 35,000 square meters. Fifteen years earlier, they had only been 15,000 square meters. Interestingly, despite the growth in store size, the range size didn't increase. The stores still held from 6,500 to around 9,000 product lines, approximately the same as 15 years earlier. The increase in store size was used to accommodate bigger sales volumes and more visitors.

Logistical Efficiency

As mentioned earlier, one important principle for Ikea has always been prioritizing logistical efficiency in the stores. There are three elements to this.

* Minimize the movement of the goods within the store. Stores are planned and the packaging of products configured so that

they can be brought directly to the sales space and sold without the need for remerchandising.

- Contrary to conventional wisdom, stock is seen as an asset, and product availability to the customer is always prioritized over stock rationalization.
- There is a belief that maximizing direct delivery from the suppliers with full utilization of the transport carriers makes economic sense.

This logic leads to greater capital expenditures in both stock and bigger stores, but the company's thinking is that there is a bigger upside in additional sales and customer satisfaction by having the goods in stock combined with higher productivity (sold goods/worked hour) through rational goods handling and lower distribution costs, made possible with bigger stores.

Generally speaking, I believe there is a risk in a short-term view of capital expenditure investments. There are a number of factors that often are not sufficiently considered. For example, it can be difficult to estimate the added benefits of logistical efficiency in project ROI calculations. Secondly, when making a new store investment decision, you can be sure that land prices will never be cheaper in the future. You can be equally sure that getting a retail license will never get easier. I think it is wise to buy as much land as you possibly can and build bigger (with a retail license) than you initially think you need to in order to ensure flexibility for the future. Finally, a project ROI calculation based on projected sales values three to five years ahead is often the norm. Given that the company is growing, this can lead to major reinvestments a few years ahead. The costs of this, combined with the business interruption, are often underestimated or not even considered in the investment request.

The risks of buying too much land or building too big stores are, at least in the Ikea case, very limited. So far I have almost never regretted building a store too big. I have, however, seen many stores that I regretted building too small. For Ikea, if a store is too big, the company has always made money by selling the land or renting out the excess building space.

CHAPTER 13

The European Expansion

The goal in Ikea's 10/10 plan was to capture a substantial share in the European and North American markets. By "a substantial share," the plan meant that Ikea should become the market leader in all European markets and reach a share of around 10 percent by 2009. At the time the plan was formulated in 1999, the country market shares ranged from 3 percent to 5 percent in most European markets outside Sweden. A commercial strategy in Europe that included aggressive price reductions and priority on the range areas of kitchen and bedroom, among other things, really paid off. In 1999, Europe contributed 80 percent of the Ikea turnover, and 10 years later, in 2009, this ratio had not changed in spite of major investments in the United States and in Asia. In the 10/10 plan, the company leadership had calculated that Europe should be down to around 75 percent by the end of the planning period.

By 2009, Ikea had a much healthier mix of countries, and dependency on a couple of markets was no longer a potential problem. I indicated earlier that back in 1983, Germany contributed 45 percent and Sweden 22 percent of Ikea's total sales. By 1995, Germany was down to 30 percent, and Sweden stood at 11 percent; in 2009, Germany's share was 16 percent and Sweden's 6 percent. Today, the UK, the United States, France, Italy, and the Netherlands are all level with or have passed Sweden in their share of company sales.

Measured by market share, by 2009, Ikea was number one in all markets in Europe with the exceptions of the UK and Austria. In the UK, the company has been hampered by very restrictive planning legislation that has prevented them from opening new stores to the extent it wants. In Austria, the market is concentrated into a few competitors with very high shares, which so far has prevented Ikea from reaching the number one position.

During these 10 years from 1999 to 2009, Ikea has seen big improvements in the former Eastern European countries Poland, the Czech Republic, and Hungary, where substantial price investments have paid off nicely. Today, these countries are contributing strongly to the sales growth and bottom line profit of the Group.

Challenges in the European Market

Looking at the competition, I don't feel Ikea has ever been seriously challenged in the European markets, at least not so far. There have been some attempts at competing against Ikea's core concept. To me, these are the least dangerous competitors. They do not come up with any innovative thinking but simply copy what Ikea has already done. So far these companies have had limited success. The traditional home furnishing competitors of earlier days have all struggled to renew themselves and are today marginal players in the market or have ceased to exist.

Some of the big DIY and hypermarket chains have tried to diversify into home furnishings. So far they seem to have met with limited success. This is not their core business—an advantage for Ikea. Ikea owns the midprice market. The exclusive high-price market is an open niche but small in volume. Low price, low quality is also free, but in my opinion it is a diminishing market. The reason for this is that consumer purchasing power is increasing. Also, low-price companies offer no price advantage to Ikea.

The midsegment traditional style is a territory not currently occupied by Ikea. This is a big market segment with the biggest likelihood of success for any European competitor to Ikea. Regarding local competition, Germany and France are the two most competitive markets for the Ikea line of business. Eastern Europe and southern Europe (Spain and Italy) are the least competitive markets. I think Ikea needs a real challenge from a global competitor in order to better itself. As we all know, lack of competition can be a powerful sleeping pill.

Dealing with Regulations

Market regulations in the European markets present a concern. In spite of the good intentions by the EU commission in its effort to make Europe more competitive, I have not seen much progress in the retail sector. Generally I believe this sector is one of the more competitive ones. If you look further back in the supply chain, you find many sectors with very limited competition. The service directive approved by the EU started with good intentions, but in the end it contained so many compromises—imposed by the individual countries of the EU—that it made little substantial difference.

Regulation concerning retail licensing is getting worse. Its effect is to prevent big retailers from expanding, thus making Europe less competitive and reducing new job opportunities. The trend is going in the wrong direction in many markets, such as France and Britain. The regulations regarding opening hours are another example of a restriction with a big impact on competitiveness and where little progress has been made toward standardization.

It's interesting to note that during the European expansion in the past 10 years, Ikea has generally been more successful when opening stores in smaller cities than in bigger ones. In the early days of the company, it focused on the main cities when expanding into new markets. Management believed that the population there was better suited for Ikea's modern style and business model. In Europe, this is no longer the case.

I think there are a few reasons for this. Most important is the lower level of competition. In smaller cities, the opening of a new Ikea store is close to the event of the year. It generates an enormous amount of free publicity and goodwill because of new job creation. An Ikea store adds to the prestige of these cities.

Also, in small cities, there is less choice and fewer alternatives for customers than in bigger cities. Therefore, the Ikea product range, with its wide scope of choice, is more competitive. It is easier to attract good employees, and customers are willing to travel farther than in bigger cities. This is an advantage, given the size of the stores where big volumes are needed to be profitable. Also, land is generally less expensive and planning is easier to get than in the big cities. Salaries are often lower, and through higher market penetration and lower costs, Ikea gets a better return on capital.

The similarities are often greater between stores in smaller cities across borders then they are between stores in bigger and smaller cities in the same country. Country borders are not always the most logical way of organizing a common range offer or common activities such as marketing or training.

CHAPTER 14

Strengthening Ikea in the United States

kea started its expansion into North America early; the first store was established in Vancouver, Canada, by 1976. Why this decision was taken I don't know—probably it was due to personal preference rather than any business logic, given the fact that Vancouver was as far away from most of Ikea's suppliers as you can get. Nevertheless, Ikea did reasonably well in Canada, and the organization there was given the directive to move across the border and establish Ikea in the United States. The first store in the United States opened in 1985 in Philadelphia.

The United States is probably the most challenging market to enter in the world today for a retail business. Back in 1985, I'm quite sure Ikea didn't know what it was getting itself into. That's probably for the best, or they might not still be there today. A strong self-confidence acquired from earlier successes in Europe meant that the company did very little research before deciding to enter this new market. Management felt that the Swedish style and the Ikea concept would work perfectly well in the United States, just as it had in other countries—including Canada. However, Ikea struggled from the start. Between 1985 and 1990, the company opened five stores on the United States East Coast and bought a competitor (STOR) on the West Coast, adding another three stores in 1992.

Having struggled for a number of years with slow sales and a loss making business, Ikea decided to stop the expansion, and no stores were opened between 1993 and 1999. For most of these years, Ikea United States barely made any money, and the business was totally focused on managing the result with low costs.

Challenges of the U.S. Market

Why is the United States such a challenge? There are a number of differences between the American and European business environments.

1. Although the home furnishing competition is relatively modest, the competition in general retail is enormous. No matter where you put a store, most customers will have to pass at least a couple of shopping malls on their way to an Ikea store.
2. The cost of doing business is high. Marketing costs are many times higher to reach the same voice share as in Europe.
3. Land and construction are more expensive than in Europe.
4. Staff costs are also higher, not least the Social Security costs. But more important, the turnover of staff is much higher compared with Europe, sometimes close to 100 percent in a year, resulting in high recruitment costs and high training costs. As a consequence, the level of competence among the staff is generally lower.
5. The home furnishing production industry is weak and not competitive. This means that most of the Ikea product range needs to be imported—the fast-moving goods mainly from Asia and furniture mainly from Europe. This leaves the company with a very vulnerable gross margin. With the rise or fall of the dollar against the euro, the gross margin could fluctuate up to 10 percentage points within a few years. The size of the country also puts pressure on overhead costs and creates additional challenges to management.

The range, however—apart from some functional adaptations (size and measurements)—needed little adjustment.

The United States in the 1990s

In 1999 and 2000, when I got close to the U.S. business and had just started as CEO, Ikea was experiencing its best years. The American economy was strong under the influence of the IT boom years, and with a strong dollar, the U.S. organization experienced a good gross margin and profitability. Ikea was affected by the dot.com collapse and a downturn in the economy in the 1990s. During much of the 1990s, the organization experienced losses or barely broke even. As a result, the self-confidence of the organization was still low. Cost cutting had been the priority for many years; there were 14 underspaced and underinvested stores with a weak range offering that was not aligned with the overall Ikea product-range strategy. The local organization believed that the Ikea wardrobes and kitchens could not be sold in the U.S. market—a major problem, since these were two of Ikea's strongest range areas in all other parts of the world. Ikea United States was a small regional player, ranked around 16 in market share.

Developing a Winning Strategy

Ikea had been preserving a malfunctioning business model for many years that didn't get the company anywhere. My view was that we had to make up our mind if we believed we could make Ikea work in America. If the answer was yes, we needed to invest strongly and get on the offensive. If no, we should close down the business and get out. The worst thing to do was to continue the same strategy, expecting the outcome to change.

Having invested in 14 stores, with a fairly high brand recognition after 15 years, we saw the potential for improvements and recognizing the potential of this big market. Ikea decided to get on the offensive: we planned to make the United States one of the future cornerstones of the company.

The company's strategy was straightforward. First of all, the U.S. product range needed to be aligned with the overall Ikea range strategy, getting the bedroom and kitchen range to take off and become the engine of the sales growth, just as they did in the rest of the Ikea markets. Next, the American organization needed to align with the wider company strategy of aggressive sales price reductions. The existing stores needed upgrading or to reestablish themselves in better locations. They had to radically reduce the turnover of staff to get a more stable working environment in the stores. The operations in the stores needed to be improved.

Most important, sales had to increase both in existing stores and through adding a substantial number of new stores. Economies of scale were important to make the numbers work. This was essential if the company was to afford necessary investments in marketing. It was needed to achieve sales volumes high enough to make it possible to build local production in the United States. The only way to get a more stable profit development over time in the United States is to source locally and thus hedge against exchange rate volatility. With margins moving up and down 10 percentage points, depending on the strength of the dollar, it was impossible to build a stable healthy profit level with only imported products.

Between 2001 and 2009, this was our goal, and we achieved it. Ikea United States moved from being a small regional company with 14 stores on the East and West coasts to developing national coverage with close to 40 stores. The company gained number two in market share, with sales moving from $1 billion in 2001 to $3 billion in 2009. Because of the severe economic downturn in the United States that began in 2008, the profit ambitions until that time had not been reached. But the first wholly owned flat line factory in the United States has been opened, and more local production is to come. The next stage of growth in the American economy, combined with increased local production, will no doubt put Ikea United States in a better position to become one of the main contributors to the Ikea results in the future.

CHAPTER 15

Developments in Russia and Asia-Pacific

T he American experience was in part similar to the European experience in the beginning of the nineties. Ikea had deviated from some of its core success criteria—the core Ikea range, aggressive pricing, and investments in the stores. But there were also some differences: the need to scale up the business to make local sourcing possible and the need to deal with different business conditions (i.e., more competition and higher costs of doing business).

In Russia the company was facing slightly different challenges. The Ikea experience in Russia is one of those classic examples of how Ikea went its own way and took substantial risk to take a major leap ahead of the competition. When all other international companies decided to leave Russia or stay out in the middle of the financial crises in the late nineties, Ikea decided to come to Russia. This was a rare opportunity to establish the company very early on in a market of the future and, given the unsettled situation in the country, acquire land in good locations at reasonable prices. This was a calculated risk. Ikea had done its math, and even if the company lost all of its investment in Russia, it would not drag down the entire company.

To meet the new challenges it was facing, Ikea also came up with a new business model. Import duties on the Ikea line of goods were, on average, 20 percent, and it was necessary to import for some time before local sourcing could be developed. At the same time, the company wanted to keep prices low, so there would be little chance of making any profit in the retail business for some years. To offset this loss, Ikea developed the shopping center concept. The idea was to build big shopping centers in connection to the stores. These centers, according to our calculations, would bring in a good profit that could help finance the loss in the Ikea stores until they were profitable. The shopping centers would be a good business on their own merits but would also bring more people to the area and consequently more visitors to the stores. The first Ikea store opened in 2000, and the first shopping center opened in 2002.

The shopping centers were a commercial success from the start. Ikea immediately established a number one position for shopping centers in Russia with a very strong mix of tenants and big visitor numbers. The return on capital in the Moscow centers was very good.

As well, the stores did better than expected. The competition and market situation in Russia, as in all emerging markets, is ideal for Ikea. On the one end, you have local small shops often with low quality and minimal design at low prices. At the other end, you have very expensive imported design furniture, affordable only for a very small group of people. At the same time, a growing middle class has limited financial means but a real need for good quality home furnishings at low prices—a perfect fit for Ikea, since no one else was equipped to fill that demand. By a stroke of luck, the Russian economy was improving, and the ruble strengthened against the dollar. The Russian Ikea organization managed to find sites and quickly build a number of stores and shopping centers. Speed was priority one, two, and three. This was a window of opportunity, and Ikea needed to get to the different cities and establish the centers before someone else did. From 2000 to 2008, the company opened 11 stores and 11 centers, in total some two million square meters and $4 billion (€2.5 billion) in investment.

This placed Ikea among the top 10 investors in Russia. Included in the investments were a distribution center and a number of Ikea-owned furniture factories. In 2009, Ikea store sales in Russia had reached almost $1.5 billion (€1 billion), 4 percent of the Group, and the stores were turning a profit.

The Future in Russia

However, there are a number of challenges that Ikea still needs to manage in order to have a solid business for the future in Russia, both for the stores and for the shopping center business. For the stores, the key question still to be resolved is how to reduce sales prices further while maintaining a reasonable margin. When entering Russia, the assumption was that this could be managed in two ways. One was that the economy would gradually be liberalized and Russia would join the World Trade Organization, thus reducing import duties. However, as yet there has not been any positive movement in that direction. Import duties are still at a 20 percent level on average.

Secondly, many people and efforts have been invested in building up local sourcing both through external suppliers and through the company's own production; this has proven much more difficult than originally anticipated. It has proven almost impossible to find able entrepreneurs who can develop competitive production. I believe this is partly due to the lack of entrepreneurial tradition in Russia and partly due to the difficult business environment, with the prevalence of bureaucracy and corruption. Unfortunately, there has been no real improvement in this area either in these last 10 years. It is evident that the Russian government is not prioritizing the furniture industry although this constitutes a fantastic opportunity to develop the Russian export industry, given the abundant existence of raw material. In fact, Ikea accounts for 40 percent of all furniture exports from Russia, even if this is a very small part of the company's global supply. Ikea owned factory investments in Russia have met many problems to develop the production.

Principally, I am an advocate of free trade and competition. But in the case of emerging markets such as Russia, I sympathize with protective measures for sectors with the potential to build up a competitive domestic industry (often linked to raw materials). It is important that these countries have a reasonable chance to reach a Western standard of living. In the short term, this will be at the expense of higher consumer prices. But this may be a price worth paying for long-term gains. In the case of Russia, it is sad that these sacrifices seem to be in vain because of domestic corruption and bureaucracy, which prevent the development of the furniture industry.

As of this writing, in 2010, I am not very optimistic about the prospects of increasing local sourcing for Ikea in Russia unless substantial improvements in the business climate occur. With its major investments and efforts, Ikea has managed to move the share of local sourcing to only 40 percent (volume) in all these years. This leaves Ikea in a difficult spot. The sales level and purchasing power differ substantially between Moscow, St. Petersburg, and the provincial cities. Sales level and purchasing power in St. Petersburg is 60 percent of what it is in Moscow, and in the provinces it is only 30 percent of what it is in Moscow. This means that sales and profits can be managed in Moscow, but the company is losing money in the provinces. This will not change until a solution is found to decrease the buying prices substantially, and there is no such solution today.

The second big challenge in Russia concerns the development of the shopping centers. Commercially, the centers have been a success, with a good tenant mix, high visitor and sale numbers, and a healthy return on capital. However, other extensive costs have been incurred that have more than offset the profits of running the business. Partly this is due to the challenging business environment in Russia, and partly it is a consequence of Ikea's priority on speed of expansion, an area in which the company has not been able to manage and control the situation properly.

Hazards of Speed

The rapid expansion into Russia left Ikea exposed to situations that have proven very costly. Many litigations and settlements with construction companies, con men, and authorities have been and still are a source of much concern in the shopping center part of the business.

There have been many changes of managers and staff, and in 2008, Ikea put on hold all new development of shopping centers and stores, except possibly in Moscow, until these problems have been solved.

The business model for the shopping centers is sound, but in my opinion there is a need to consolidate the business and get to a point of profitability before moving on. The business model for the stores needs a solution to the sourcing problems before new stores can be justified. I do hope a solution will be found eventually because the company is well placed to build a successful business in Russia.

Ikea in Asia-Pacific

In the "Ten Jobs in Ten Years (10/10)" direction, Ikea stated, "In Asia-Pacific, the big challenge will be to gain a strong foothold in the countries we have already chosen to enter and to get to a point of profitability." In 1999, Ikea's presence in Asia-Pacific was marginal. There were in total six very small stores, more like start-up shops: four in Australia and two in China. They were sourced from a central warehouse in Malaysia, where the Asia-Pacific central office was located. The stores were, of course, all unprofitable.

Asia-Pacific had the potential of becoming a third leg in the Ikea geographical strategy together with Europe and North America. The long-term growth prospects were evident.

What was the best strategy going forward? Again it was a question of doing things the way they should have been implemented from the start: building big Ikea concept stores where the full power of the product range—as well as other services such as the restaurant and children's ball room—could be provided. It was also important to find a way to compete with lower prices and at the same time be profitable.

The answer again was found in building sufficient economies of scale to achieve the right level of leverage in the supply chain. To make that happen, at least two big markets were needed. China was an evident candidate, but it would take time to build up sufficient sales volumes, given the low purchasing power and low sales prices needed. The answer was to complement China with Japan, where it was possible to immediately get high sales-volume stores. The close proximity of these two markets was helpful. To be able to offer competitive prices and good product availability in the stores, it was necessary to build up local sourcing and a central warehouse hub in China.

The regional office was moved from Singapore, Malaysia, to Shanghai. A central warehouse was built in Shanghai and complemented with local warehouses in Australia and Japan. Local sourcing was of course much easier to establish in China than in Russia. A structure with buying offices was already in place that now had to work with both global sourcing and local sourcing for the region. There was an advantage in not hurrying, as had been the case in Russia. There was no specific timing opportunity in China, and the company could develop its business in an orderly way.

In Australia, with a supply chain structure in place, the answer was simple: since Australia is similar to the European markets, replace the small shops with big Ikea stores and run them efficiently. This was done, and Ikea is now turning a healthy profit in Australia.

Japan, on the other hand, represented a new experience, presenting challenges the company had not encountered before. On the positive side, Japan is a very big market with high purchasing power and population density. The competition was fragmented and very traditional, with few international companies present and high sales prices. The Ikea style was well suited to Japanese tastes. At the time of Ikea's arrival, Japan was also experiencing a change in social values; the company's unique concept and values could fit well into this change.

Significant Obstacles

There were some challenges, of course. Land prices in Japan are very high. With an interest rate of almost zero, this wasn't a short-term problem, but it represented a potential risk for the future. The demands on service and quality are very high, and it was uncertain to what extent customers would accept Ikea's self-serve concept.

The Japanese culture also felt very alien to a Swedish company, and it was difficult to know how well Ikea's values would fit with it. This was a significant consideration when hiring Japanese managers.

The biggest challenge was Japanese restrictions on the formaldehyde level in furniture products. The accepted level in Japan was half that accepted in other markets. This meant that several hundred of the most important Ikea products would have to be produced specifically for the Japanese market at a buying price 20 percent higher than what Ikea would normally pay. In the short term, this could be handled, but long term that price level would be impossible to maintain. The company had to find a solution before deciding to enter the Japanese market.

The solution was a typical Ikea one. Turn the problem into an opportunity! The company started a project intended to reduce the formaldehyde content of the products to the Japanese level but without increasing costs. The thinking was that sooner or later the legislated levels would become stricter in other markets too; this gave Ikea an opportunity to find a solution well in advance without being under time pressure. This would also demonstrate the company's commitment to the environment. A solution was found, and today the Japanese norm for formaldehyde is the norm for all Ikea products—and it is on the way to becoming the new furniture industry standard.

The first Japanese store was opened in 2006. Until 2009, five stores had been opened, three in the Tokyo area, one in Kobe, and one in Osaka. Overall, the Ikea offering, the store concept, and the prices have worked well in Japan. The one concern is the low level of home furnishing consumption per capita in Japan. A lot of hard work needs to be put into increasing the interest in home furnishings. By 2009, sales were approaching $570.6 million (€400 million), and Ikea turned a healthy profit.

The Situation in China

In China, the challenges were different. Compared to Russia, the general business environment in China is easier to deal with. In my experience, the Chinese authorities are cooperative, decisive, and in general are genuinely willing to do things that are in the best interest of their people. However, there is intense competition among businesses in China on price, and the size of the country and the size of the population combined with low purchasing power pose a number of hurdles. Buying in China is easy, but selling there is a real challenge.

Key to success was the company's sourcing strategy. Sales prices had to be reduced by at least 50 percent from the initial level when much of the sourcing came from Europe. To achieve 50 percent lower prices, local sourcing and very large volumes were necessary. In 2009, more than 50 percent of the sales volume sold in China was sourced in that country. Sales prices had been reduced according to the plan. Going forward, Ikea's big effort in sourcing in China will be to grapple with product quality and the working conditions at the suppliers.

In China, the company had to adjust not only the supply strategy but also some components of the commercial strategy in order to succeed. Lower sales prices meant that the product volumes going through the stores were much higher than normal. On top of that, store visitor numbers were much higher than Ikea was used to. The stores had to be built to accommodate these high volumes. Simply building larger stores was not an acceptable solution; land in China is as expensive or sometimes more expensive than in Western countries.

Ikea's solution was a store concept in which the showroom and market hall were both placed on top of the warehouse for a total of three floors rather than the usual two. This way, bigger volumes could be brought in without having to buy more land.

Another area where new thinking was needed was the Ikea rule of mass distribution of the company catalog to all households in the catchment area. Given the vast numbers of people living around the Chinese stores, a more selective method was needed. The product range also needed some adaptation. To address this issue, the company applied a bigger range in the low price segment.

The business model in China now works, and Ikea can be competitive and profitable. In 2010, there were nine stores in China, and more stores can now be rolled out at a quicker pace.

By 2009, the three countries Australia, Japan, and China together were approaching a sales level of $1.4 billion (€1 billion), and all were profitable. A solid strategy is in place with a strong team. The potential is there to make these markets a growth engine for Ikea for many years to come. The 10/10 plan to gain a strong foothold and reach a level of profitability in Asia-Pacific by 2009 had been achieved.

CHAPTER 16

A Local Company or a Global Retailer?

Becoming a successful global retailer is, of course, an exciting ambition for any company. However with increasing size and recognition come some potential disadvantages. To many people, global business presents threats:

- The threat that small companies will be pushed out of business
- The threat that global companies will exploit poor people in developing countries
- The threat that big business in general is too powerful

In the eyes of the customers, the local connection of companies is important. I think it is important for big global retailers not to ignore this. Having an identity, a heritage, and being locally connected should be an important part of the values and strategy of any company.

The Local Connection

Is Ikea really a Swedish company with a local touch? Or is it a big anonymous global retailer? The founder lives in Switzerland. The head office is in the Netherlands. The owner is a Dutch foundation. Less than 10 percent of the employees work in Sweden. Sweden contributes only 7 percent of total sales and 5 percent of buying, and this will decrease even more in the future. In fact, with only 7 percent of sales coming from the home market, Ikea is probably one of the most international retail chains in the world.

So what gives Ikea its distinctively Swedish character? Three things in my opinion: the heritage, the values and management style, and the product range. This is backed up by the blue and yellow stores (the colors of the Swedish national flag) and the restaurants, which serve Swedish food.

- **The heritage.** I think it is very important for companies to have a history and a soul. The heart of Ikea is found in the soil of the Swedish county Småland, the area where the founder Ingvar Kamprad grew up. The history and the character of the founder explain how Ikea became what it is and put a human face on the company.
- **The values and management style.** This is the glue that holds the company together. Ikea's values reflect those of Kamprad, but I think they also have much to do with how many outsiders view Swedish managers and management style.
- **The product range.** Ikea's founding documents state that in Scandinavia, the product range shall be seen as typical Ikea, and outside Scandinavia, it shall be seen as typical Swedish. The Swedish range expression is one of the company's important competitive advantages. It separates Ikea from furniture retailers in all markets. But it is not only the style of the product range but also the way the interiors in the stores are furnished and how the room sets in the catalog reflect a Swedish way of living.

Maintaining the "Swedish" and Local Character

Ikea will in the years to come become even more global regarding markets, employees, and sales. That is unavoidable with continued growth, and it will mandate an even greater need to strengthen its Swedish character. "Swedishness" is a competitive edge with respect to range, values, and heritage. This I think can be achieved. A greater challenge will be to create the local touch. For this to happen, store managers must have a greater mandate to make decisions and preferably be locally grounded—that is, to live and be active in the local community.

I think any global retailer should try to establish a clear heritage and local connection. Being global is positive only to a portion of the company's stakeholders, such as shareholders and the financial market. To the customers and many other stakeholders, the local character of the company will probably become more and more important. Local companies usually have a stronger community presence. They can make decisions about sponsorships, charity, and other local contributions, and people perceive they have a long-term commitment to the community. Being a good corporate citizen can only partly be achieved through big charity programs and sponsorships managed at the corporate level. For the majority of people, I believe the local contribution is more important in establishing the company as a responsible corporate citizen.

CHAPTER 17

Global Expansion in Retail

Globalization in the big box retailing sector has had mixed results over the past few years. Ten years ago when I looked at the competition Ikea was facing, I was certain we would see a surge of international expansion from the big retailers of this world. Many certainly tried, but the results have been mixed. Very few big European retailers have been successful in the United States. Very few big American retailers have been successful in Europe. The U.S. giant Home Depot abandoned its international ambitions a few years ago. Walmart made an unsuccessful attempt to enter into Germany. Carrefour left Japan, Thailand, Malaysia, and Russia. European companies seem to expand mainly to neighboring countries or Eastern Europe and Russia, while U.S. companies stay in North and South America. Japan is still unexplored by most. And we haven't seen any new big retailers coming out of the emerging markets. Why is this? Global sourcing has taken off, but global selling through own outlets has not.

Looking at the Ikea experience can give some hints. First of all, to be really successful in global expansion, you need to offer something unique, something the local competition cannot match. For big box retailers in sectors such as hypermarkets, electronics, or DIY, the offerings are, in most cases, very similar, and there is little differentiation when moving to other Western countries. In emerging markets, however, the "Western" offer sometimes stands a chance of being unique.

Another difficulty is that the most likely scenario when entering most emerging markets is many years of low or no profitability and a high level of risk before you can harvest. This is probably less appealing to investors and management in many publicly owned companies who are looking for superior returns in the shorter term.

A third challenge is that many of the big retailers have limited experience in operating overseas. Not least, cultural differences seem to be a large obstacle for many.

But the internal limitations of companies is only one aspect preventing progress in retail globalization. I do have some concerns about the general development of free competitive market economies. Progress is slow, and in some cases I even feel the trend negative. Most business people, I think, subscribe to a belief in free competition. Strangely, though, there seems to be ample evidence of many businesses doing their utmost to limit free competition. From time to time, the media highlights blatant price fixing, but more common are more subtle arrangements to avoid price competition.

For instance, some brand owners try to control their customers' retail prices, or retailers avoid active price competition to keep margins at a good level. This is all to the detriment of the consumer and companies trying to compete. In many business sectors, consolidation is an important trend, with the consequence of more limited competition. Oligopoly, at best, is common in many sectors. This, of course, makes entry into new markets more difficult.

Interference by the Government

Governments and politicians also say they want more free competition. But in many markets, we see more and more examples of various trade barriers being introduced, extended, or prolonged. Ikea has confronted trade barriers such as import duties (in Russia), product specifications (formaldehyde in Japan), bureaucracy and corruption (Russia again), trade licensing (many European countries), and currency fluctuations (United States and Russia). All these are good examples of challenges preventing global expansion.

The political situation within a country is sometimes an important aspect of a new market entry. What principles should guide such decisions? I have always been of the opinion that following the United Nations directives on this matter is as good a yardstick as any. Operating in countries where democracy is not yet fully developed is often the best way to influence progress. Avoiding such countries can promote isolation.

On a similar note, should we say no to production in areas where child labor is common? This is the easy way out if you want to avoid headlines in Western media. However, we will, in my opinion, do more to eradicate child labor if we are present and can influence working conditions with our policies, actions, and values. In most cases, to engage and show a good example is better than isolation or avoidance. I do sincerely believe this; it is not an excuse to do business. If we want to support developing countries, we must be present.

One of the most difficult challenges when entering new markets is corruption. This may be the biggest threat to global retail as well as to growth in general in developing countries. During my years at Ikea, I didn't see much evidence of improvements in this area. As we all know, corruption is rampant in many developing countries. But in the economies of Western nations, more and more evidence of corruption is coming to light, both in the public and private sectors.

If you categorically say no to corruption (which we must), it is impossible to operate in many countries, provided that your business depends on decisions and permissions from authorities. This is a real threat to globalization. Too little attention and work is, in my opinion, going into reducing corruption and discussing how to handle it from a business perspective. This subject ought to be higher on the agenda of international organizations and governments.

Prospects for Future Business

What will happen in the coming years? Many of the obstacles and challenges as described above will probably remain.

In most European countries and the United States, we will see low GDP growth, an aging population, and household spending shifting toward telecommunication, IT, medical, and energy and away from home furnishings, fashion, DIY, and other traditional retail sectors. Growth will depend on beating the competitors, not on expanding the market. The best will survive in increasingly consolidated markets. Organic growth will be difficult with present and new restrictions in many markets. With increasing consolidation, competition authorities will increasingly question potential acquisitions.

Many of the big Western retailers operating on thin margins will be busy defending their home turf. In this environment, it will be even more important for Western retailers to learn how to grow in emerging markets. This will quite possibly be more important than many think today. Many Western companies with a low share in emerging markets will need a significant growth in these markets to see an impact on the overall growth of their companies.

An important next step in global retail will come if and when foreign ownership rules are liberated for retailing in India. This will be an interesting opportunity for many of today's successful global retailers. However, today there is little evidence that this will happen anytime in the near future. Outside the obvious BRIC countries, I am sure we will also see a number of new interesting emerging markets on the horizon. Countries such as Egypt, Turkey, Mexico, and Vietnam all have the potential to be big-growth markets.

Who will be the first successful global retailer emerging from a developing country? This will be an interesting challenge for the established global retailers of today.

Being successful as a truly global retailer is a challenge. The different situations of Europe, North America, Asia, Russia, and other markets as discussed above have proven very demanding for many retailers. Some important criteria for success include:

- Being able to adapt the offer to fit different markets while remaining unique

- Being able to have competitive prices, especially in emerging markets
- Having a strong value base that can fit in very different cultures
- Having an approach to new markets where the company is seen to contribute in other ways than just enriching itself
- Being able to take risks and accept low or no profit for a number of years in future growth markets

It's also important to have a strong profitable home base that can finance this. Not many of today's big retailers seem to be in that position.

PART 4

Building for the Long Term

What kind of ownership or governance is needed to be a successful business contributing to a better society? As I have elaborated on throughout the text, there are a number of principles and behaviors that I think are important and need to be established and promoted by the owner or owners: long-term thinking, a willingness to take risks, balanced remuneration of managers, establishing a history and a heritage, strong sound values, and a vision that speaks to all stakeholders.

Are there any potential downsides to being private or public with a committed founder or owner in control as opposed to being public with a differentiated and anonymous owner structure? I cannot think of very many.

It's true that private companies can suffer from a lack of transparency and potential negative publicity as a consequence. They also have more limited financing than public companies. The most important downside is probably related to those companies that are 100 percent privately owned and where important employees cannot acquire or sell a stake in the company at a well-established market value. The motivation of ownership should not be underestimated.

Advantages of Strong Owner Control

I see many advantages of strong owner control. In such companies, it's more likely that the business will have a longer-term perspective and be willing to take more risks. Both these factors are likely to bring more fundamental change or provide greater opportunities to move ahead of the competition.

The existence of a present, dedicated, and knowledgeable founder and owner is also a considerable advantage. The founder is crucial to establishing the strong heritage and values that give the company a soul by which loyalty and motivation among the employees can more easily be created. No employed CEO will stay long enough to be able to take on that role.

With their competence and knowledge, owners can both challenge management and restrain the company from excesses in perks and compensation. I also think the likelihood of being a "good company" is greater with a strong owner in charge. Profits can be deployed to good causes without much debate. In my opinion, private companies or publicly owned companies with one committed controlling shareholder have better prerequisites in place to create competitiveness, a dedicated workforce, and good citizenship than do public companies with a diluted ownership structure. This is, of course, predicated on the founder or owner having the wisdom, dedication, knowledge, leadership, and values required.

There is, however, one form of private ownership that in my opinion has difficulties living up to the criteria above: private equity. That is for the simple reason that private equity companies have two fundamental objectives that do not align with my thinking of success: One is to exit within a short time frame (5 to 7 years). Another is to satisfy only one stakeholder, the owners. Therefore, I believe it is very difficult for private-equity-owned companies to take necessary risks, take a long-term view, develop a strong heritage and values—the soul of the company—and contribute to a better society encompassing many different stakeholders.

The Challenge of a Publicly Held Company

What is the destiny of public companies with widely distributed ownership? Is the situation hopeless? Are they doomed to short term-ism, poor financial performance, and bad reputations? Of course, it is not as black and white as that. There are privately controlled companies with bad reputations and results, and there are public companies that are doing well.

Ideally, managers and board members in public companies should act as if they own the company. Is there any evidence to support this hypothesis? One comparison made by a Swedish newspaper in 2010—comparing listed companies with owners holding less than 10 percent of the company's shares with the average of the Swedish stock exchange index OMXS and the small company index CSX (predominantly companies with majority owners) from 2002 to 2010—showed an index development of 196 for the group of no majority owners, 226 for OMXS, and 261 for CSX.

The Structure of Ikea

Ikea is a private company, or, to be more accurate, Ikea is a Dutch foundation. This company structure was put in place in 1982. The main purpose as explained by the founder Ingvar Kamprad was to secure Ikea's future by removing the risk of being split up or sold by later generations. A second purpose, though probably less important, may have been to create a tax-efficient structure. The mother company is INGKA Holding B.V., which is owned by the Stichting INGKA Foundation, which in turn is owned by the Ikea Foundation. The statutes of the foundation state that donations should be given to architectural and interior design innovations.

Much of the criticism of Ikea over the years has been linked to this company setup and its lack of transparency. Being a private company, INGKA Holding B.V. has little legal obligation to inform or explain financial results, ownership, and organization structures. The information strategy chosen by the founder has been to say as little as possible. As a result, Ikea has presented itself to the public as a very secretive company. This has raised suspicions that there is something to hide. Speculation centers on the question of Ikea's tax policies, if the founder is getting rich—in spite of saying he isn't—and if Ikea is the good citizen it claims to be. Some attempts have been made over the years to analyze the structure; perhaps the best or most accurate of which I have seen was published in *The Economist* in 2006.

Looking at these issues as objectively as I can, I would say that Ikea is tax efficient. The tax paid by INGKA Holding B.V. has been around 25 percent for many years; by 2008, it had come down to around 20 percent. These accounts are public knowledge and are examined by the media from time to time. Tax is paid by local Ikea companies in each country of operation, just as it should be. However, the average tax rate is no doubt lower than many retail companies pay. This is mainly due to the fact that Ikea operates its wholesale company from Switzerland and its treasury func tion from a service company in Belgium, both of which are very tax efficient. However, this is by no means unusual among other companies, many of which have similar structures. So in my opin ion, this is not overly tax aggressive. The fact that taxes have been reduced further the past few years is more a function of lower tax rates generally in many countries and the sales and profit mix of Ikea countries. That companies choose to have their operations in countries with better tax rates is part of keeping costs low. Countries choose to compete with each other over tax rates, and companies respond to that. The important thing is that taxes are paid where the company operates.

Good Corporate Citizenship

Is Ikea meeting its responsibility as a good citizen? The answer to that question depends on how you define "taking responsibility." My view is that Ikea is a responsible company in terms of how it conducts its business—how it acts toward its different stakehold-ers. However, if "taking responsibility" refers to the company's or the owner's contributions to charitable causes, you could probably argue that more could be done.

A problem has been the limitations of the statutes of the Ikea Foundation. Because the foundation is limited to funding archi-tecture or interior design, this creates a problem for those who want to use the foundation for good causes. One way to deal with this has been to finance many projects from Ikea companies rather than from the foundation. Important steps have been taken to change the purpose of the foundation to make it possible to support good causes in a less specific and limited way. When this is achieved, I think we will see much bigger contributions from the Ikea Foundation.

That being said, I have to admit to mixed feelings about the debate that sometimes exists in the media regarding charity. When wealthy people or organizations contribute to charitable causes, this is, of course, excellent in most cases. This is particularly true if the charity is focused on activities that help bring poor people to a level of employability. Health care and education are the two most obvious examples. However, I disagree with the view that those who give the most are the "best." This may be the case if the wealth accumulated and donated has been acquired in an appropriate way—meaning that the business behind the fortunes was conducted in a sustainable, responsible way, taking all stakeholders into consideration. It may be also the case if the company behind the fortunes has reinvested its earnings and grown the business to the limits of what is possible, since I believe that growing a business in a responsible way will contribute more to society than giving away the proceeds to charity.

We should also consider these aspects when evaluating and recognizing present and former business owners' contributions to society. Also worth taking into account when recognizing donations to good causes are the wise words of Mohandas Gandhi: "It is not how much we give, but how much of what we have that we give that determines the level of our commitment."

Difficulties of Franchising

The weak spot in the Ikea organizational structure in my opinion is the franchise system. Again, this is perfectly normal in the sense that there are many franchise systems that operate like the franchisor Inter Ikea Systems. However, this can be seen as being overly smart and tax aggressive, given that the top companies in Inter Ikea, which receive 3 percent of Ikea sales a year in franchise fees, are based in "tax havens" (as published in *The Economist*). Maybe this system was too clever. Tax havens were not as criticized and scrutinized at the time when this structure was put into place, but given the development in society where more and more transparency is demanded, I think it would be best to communicate more openly about this.

Is Ingvar Kamprad privately taking money out of the system through this structure? Well, I don't know for sure, of course, but I don't think so. He may control more assets than he has led us to believe, but my guess is that these assets are dedicated to the company. Having known him for so long, I am certain that his only concern is to do what is best for Ikea.

The best way to get rid of negative speculations would be more openness about what happens to the money in Inter Ikea. That way the company would align itself better to the development of our society with demands for more transparency.

Ikea has a dedicated founder. I have been very fortunate to be given the privilege to know and work with Kamprad for 20 years, starting as his assistant in 1988. He has never ceased to amaze me with his devotion to Ikea, his tremendous intuition; his enormous willpower, energy, and consistency; his unique ability not to let his success and fortunes corrupt him; his caring and humorous nature; and his ability to turn problems into opportunities—the list is endless. I am very proud of the trust he put in me when I was given the job as CEO in 1999.

However, there is a flip side to every coin. Kamprad's love for Ikea—his unwillingness to let go, his view that he is the only one who really understands what is best for Ikea—is a hindrance to a smooth transition on the day he (reluctantly) must pass the baton on to the next generation. A big man casts a big shadow under which it is sometimes difficult to grow. However, I am hopeful. I think Ikea is both ready and willing to take that responsibility. I feel the Ikea people have shown that they can make the right decisions and lead the organization on their own.

There are a couple of risks in that transition that must be dealt with. The most important is a gradual weakening of the Ikea values and vision as guiding stars for the company. Ingvar Kamprad has always been the strong guardian of this, and Ikea must make sure that someone from the founder's family takes on that responsibility. A second problem is how to secure a strong, trustful, and clear relationship between the three important bodies: the founding family, the INGKA board, and management. They all have important roles to fulfill, and common ground must be found where all can interact in a strong way and create clarity and motivation in the organization. If that can be achieved, there is no doubt in my mind that Ikea has the ability to continue to grow and prosper for many years to come.

Looking to the Future

Ikea is still a first-generation company, and the test of succession has yet to be passed. What is the best way to achieve a successful transfer of ownership from one generation to the next? In my own country, Sweden, we have seen many good examples where the next generations of the founder's relatives have successfully managed to grow and develop their companies. Hennes & Mauritz (H&M), Axel Johnson AB, the Bonnier Group, and the Wallenberg controlled companies are all majority-owned and have been led by the same families for generations.

These companies set good examples, and they are very important to the Swedish society. A common denominator for these companies is that the succeeding generations have had able and dedicated individuals who have been willing to lead the company both as CEOs and owners. I believe that the best solution is when the next generations are able to take an operational responsibility (CEO) as well as an owner role. This must, of course, be based upon meritocracy. To understand the business and, even more important, to build relationships, loyalty, and trust with employees, you need to be firmly integrated in the business. This way, you are not only in charge of the business agenda but also in a position to strengthen the values and vision of the company. You can inherit the financial assets, but the loyalty and respect of the employees, the most important assets of the company, must be earned by every generation.

If this is not possible, a second-best option is a dedicated, involved owner who works in a strong relationship with a hired CEO. It is preferable that the operational head of the company be internally groomed, possessing a deep competence and sharing the values of the company's founder.

Now, all this is fairly evident. But what do you do when there are no relatives with an interest and/or ability to lead the company? The founder must then decide if his or her priority is the best interest of the company and its stakeholders, his or her own reputation, or securing the financial independence of future generations of relatives. My own preference would be the first option, because securing the continued growth of the company, I believe, will be most beneficial to society at large.

This would mean that the priority in this case is to find an able leader and entrepreneur who is given the opportunity to acquire a majority stake in the company (if necessary, at a discounted price). I am sure this is a very difficult and emotional decision for the founder to make, but it is a necessary one.

If, as the founder, your priority is your own reputation, you can, of course, sell the company to the highest bidder and donate the proceeds to charitable causes. If members of future generations have a good idea what to do with their inheritance—that is, start another company—you may well be justified in selling the company and turning the profits over to them. But my own opinion is that giving fortunes away to relatives may be the worst thing you can do to them. You are robbing them of one of life's greatest joys— to succeed on your own, providing for yourself and your family, and having a meaningful life through hard and stimulating work. I can say only that I am happy I don't have to make these choices. Founders of successful businesses may find neither alternative attractive. You are damned if you do and damned if you don't.

Challenges of a Charitable Foundation Structure

On a last note, is a charitable foundation structure, such as the one Ikea has adopted, the best way to safeguard the future of a company? I am not sure. In a situation with different opinions among the heirs about what to do with the company, or where one or more of them are willing and able to succeed the founder, it may be a good structure to ensure that the company remains intact. If all the heirs are able and willing and in agreement about taking over the company, this structure probably has no significant advantages from the perspective of how to run the company in the best way.

The problems occur when no relative is willing or able to take responsibility for the future of the company. Then Ikea's charitable foundation structure has the potential to create a bad marriage. On the one hand, you have an owner with limited interest in the company, holding a grudge because the foundation is unable to release the heritage. On the one hand, there are managers and board members with no ownership opportunity in the company. In a situation like this, a foundation structure may be the formula for the destruction of the company rather than its preservation. The best advice seems to be: keep your options open until you have a fair idea what the ambitions and competence of the next generation will be.

CHAPTER 18

The Financials

When discussing financial policies and thinking, there is no one-size-fits-all approach. The type of business you are in and your earnings and cash generation potential set the scene for all your actions. A successful business model in combination with private ownership does, however, create a level of freedom to use capital that can create additional advantages. A number of lessons can be learned from the Ikea case that can be of interest to companies in similar situations.

P&L and Balance Sheets

Ikea's approach to profit and loss statements and balance sheets is a bit different from many other retailers. Contrary to other business decisions, this is an area in which the company is risk averse and maintains a very conservative approach. Under no circumstances does Ikea want to jeopardize its independence as a company. Had profits been lower than they have been, this would certainly have meant less capital investments and, as a consequence, a slower growth pace.

The most important policy is that the money must be earned before it is spent! This is not always a common policy among other businesses. It is also the company's policy to always own the property on which its stores are located as well as the stores themselves. Ikea does not want to be at the mercy of landlords and wants to control rental levels itself. Owning instead of renting has other advantages. Stores can be changed or updated whenever needed, and the company retains the opportunity of capital gains itself. It is also the policy to hold minimum 12 percent of revenues in net cash. If the economy is in a downturn, Ikea the company can make its own choices and realize investment opportunities when they occur without being dependent on financial institutions. Ikea also maintains restrictive policies regarding financing; money is borrowed only for construction of property.

The company takes a long-term view on investments and usually buys more land and builds larger stores than necessary in the mid-term in order to be able to expand easily in the future. The view is that land and construction will never be cheaper than they are today. The company also takes the view that product stock really is an asset; thus Ikea tends to prioritize product availability and logistical efficiency over minimizing stock levels. The policy is also to pay suppliers on time, often within 30 days—an unusual standard in the retail industry. It is likely that this results in lower purchase prices; most definitely it results in happier suppliers. Thus, minimizing working capital is certainly not a priority.

Controlling Its Own Destiny

I suppose this leaves Ikea with a balance sheet that looks a little odd to most retail companies with a sales/assets ratio well below one. But since Ikea is a private company, it need not concern itself with maximizing shareholder value in the short term. This policy gives Ikea greater security and the ability to control its own destiny.

A policy like this, of course, relies on high levels of profitability consistently over many years, especially when you are a private company such as Ikea. So far the company has been able to deliver profits enough to finance yearly investments on a level of around $4.3 billion (€3 billion) in 2009. Being privately held can, of course, be a constraint on financing, but it also can provide an opportunity. There is very little pressure to pay dividends to the owner (the Ikea Foundation) if the capital is needed to expand the business. For me as CEO, for our management, and for our employees, it was always very comforting to know that the profits stayed within the firm and were reinvested into the business.

Turning to the profit and loss statement, priorities one, two, and three are sales. Ikea is very sales-growth driven. This derives from the company's vision: to serve the majority of people. And it derives from a business model and financing policy that imply a high level of fixed costs. Because of this, it is necessary to grow sales volume in order to be cost efficient and reach a good profit level. With a pricing policy that does not merely match the competition or barely undercuts it but creates a substantial price difference, there is also a need for a very efficient supply chain to finance these sales price investments and deliver reasonable margins. Finally, the cost focus is always primarily on staff costs. Staff make up about 40 percent of costs, and with the challenge of managing both salary inflation and sales price reductions, ideally up to 10 percent productivity improvements per year are needed to reduce the cost ratio. This is something the company has not achieved during the past few years.

From a CEO's perspective, making no comments on questions about financial information was mostly positive. Once you do, it is the only thing the press wants to talk about. Ikea prefers to talk about home furnishings, its products, and other things of relevance to the general public. Satisfying the curiosity of the financial community is of no interest to Ikea. The people who need to know (the financial partners) get the information they need.

That said, some sort of limited information about the annual results, including a short statement, would probably serve Ikea better and help build a reputation as a transparent, open, and honest company. Stubbornly refusing to say anything sends a strange message. Lack of transparency raises unnecessary suspicions that the company is hiding something. A change in the company policy regarding publicizing financial information occurred in 2010.

CHAPTER 19

The Role of the CEO

What is the role of the CEO? I am sure this can be described in many ways. My simplest definition of a CEO's function would be to lead the process of development and make recommendations to the board regarding:

- The vision and objectives (the ambition level)
- The strategies (how to get there)
- The value system, the organization, governance structure, and policies (the framework)
- Budgets (allocation of resources)

Steps to Successful Leadership

With those decisions in place, the responsibility is then to recruit the people to do it and provide the leadership to make it happen. Some of this has already been discussed in more detail, but let me give some additional reflections on some of these things.

Set Very Challenging Objectives

This has the effect of opening eyes to see new possibilities. It touches people and creates energy and motivation. Sometimes people will complain that these objectives are unrealistic, but good people most often respond very well to very challenging objectives. It is amazing how often what seems unachievable actually does happen when you set your mind to it. When ambitious goals fail, it is probably more often poor execution that is the problem than the goal itself.

Setting soft goals, to me, is managing, not leading. Leading is giving your people the opportunity to stretch themselves to the limits of their potential, not just mandating them to do their jobs. For instance, in Ikea:

- We said we would triple sales in 10 years.
- We said we would reduce sales and buying prices by 20 percent in 10 years.
- We said we would reduce our country organizations by 50 percent.
- We said we would aim for 100 percent renewable energy.

These types of goals require a different mind-set, one that helps to trigger real change.

Create Directions and Strategies

I am in favor of a fairly long-time perspective when it comes to planning. For one thing, I feel it triggers bigger ambitions; secondly, with a shorter-time perspective, the risk is that you spend too much time planning and leave too little time for execution. I used a 10-year framework for the company direction (10/10).

You may say that 10 years is too long. It does not create a sense of urgency. You will not see the end of it yourself, and circumstances change too fast for such a long time perspective. Yes, maybe, but on the other hand, some things require a long time to fundamentally change. A longer time perspective creates security and stability in the organization. Too often I have seen managers create frustration and insecurity with endless changes in direction and organizational structure. And of course 10 years is an arbitrary number; it is the perspective that matters. Reaching out all the way in an organization the size of Ikea (125,000 employees) and achieving fundamental change takes time. That plans are too short lived to have a real effect, I believe, is more common than that they are too long.

Create a Useful Organizational Structure

I am a believer in organizations that support cooperation across functions. Define your main business processes—in Ikea's case, they're the supplying process, the creating demand process, and the selling and communicating process—and then create an organizational structure that supports this way of working. This is not easy because you need to organize according to function (i.e., buying, distribution, production, range development, and retail stores) but also make sure you can work in process.

Secondly, I am a believer in flat organizations. The more hierarchies or organizational levels there are, the more bureaucracy and less responsibility for the individual there is. At Ikea, when the increase in size called for new organizational levels—for example, at a regional level—I always refused to add regional organizations. A regional manager, yes, if necessary, but never a regional organization.

If possible, regional managers should also have a dual responsibility, such as country manager or store manager. As a consequence, contrary to conventional wisdom, I prefer big control spans for managers (the number of people that report to a particular manager). Smaller spans of control can be good in certain situations, like when you are in a crisis, when the competence of the people working for you is low, or when close control is your preferred leadership style. Then you need to have close and frequent dialogue with your people.

Having many people reporting to you, on the other hand, reduces the number of organizational levels and gives more freedom to the people working for you. You simply don't have the time to be in constant contact with them. This works well when you and your employees have a clear, common view on values, objectives, and strategies; you trust each other; the level of competence is high; and your own leadership style is one of support rather than control. Most competent people do not want their managers on their backs all the time. They want the freedom to get on with their assignments. You should be there for them when they need you. You should give them support. And of course you should set high demands.

This has nothing to do with abdicating responsibility. I think some managers equate hard work and doing their job with knowing everything and being in control of everything all the time. My experience is that this is not what competent people need. As CEO, you should give support and ensure the things agreed happen, but you must also have the time to think about what to do next.

Build a Strong Governance Structure

Some people prefer small management teams, meeting frequently (weekly or monthly), where all or most decisions are made. The good thing about this way of working is that everyone in the team is updated on what is going on, and it is clear to the organization where decisions are made.

I myself have never worked with that model. The downside of it, in my opinion, is that the key managers risk spending too much time in meetings, becoming absorbed in very operational and short-term issues. Because most decisions are channeled to this group, there is also the risk of a bottleneck.

My preference has been to have a fairly big executive team that meets only a few times a year (maybe five times for two days) for longer-term planning and reflection. The team then delegates most of the shorter-term decision making to committees. A big executive team gives more people the chance to understand the total business and thus promote cooperative thinking, and fewer meetings give each member of the team more time for their individual responsibilities.

The use of committees makes it possible to separate the decisions related to the execution of the strategies and plans (in the committees) and the decisions related to longer-term planning (the less-frequent executive meetings). The committees include executive members relevant to the subject and other managers important for the execution. Thus you ensure that expertise is part of the decision making, and you get the buy-in needed for good execution.

The downside of this way of working is that people in the organization can be confused about where different decisions are made.

Recruit the Right People

How high you set the bar when recruiting will determine how successful you will be. Lower demands equal lower results; higher demands bring higher results. When in doubt, do not recruit, even if you are under pressure to fill a vacancy. Most of the time, your gut feeling is correct. External recruitment, in most cases, should be the last resort.

What do I look for in a manager? Energy, perseverance, commitment, results, values, integrity, cooperation, potential to develop people, and potential to develop the business through specialist competence. The ideal manager combines a high level of energy, social competence, and professional skills. All three are equally important.

Some Thoughts on Good Leadership

Developing my leadership style has been an ongoing process during my entire working life. For a long time, it was a very unconscious process. During a period when I was younger, I tried to understand leadership by looking at others and reading books about leadership. This was quite overwhelming. So much wisdom, so many ideas. It created in me a sense of insufficiency and frustration. Living up to the requirements of a good leader seemed unachievable.

Here are some truths that have helped me get a foothold on my leadership and feel okay about it:

- There is no such thing as a perfect leader or role model. Different situations and different people require different types of leadership.
- Being charismatic is not necessary to be a good leader.
- Developing my leadership comes from understanding myself, my own strengths and weaknesses, and building on them rather than trying to copy others or to follow the advice of experts.

Good leaders, to me, are those who have managed to help me feel motivated and energized over a longer period of time. What is it, then, that triggers motivation?

The way I see it, motivation comes from satisfying one's needs. On a very basic level, for instance, when you are hungry, you are motivated to eat. When you are tired, you are motivated to sleep. I believe that the path to good leadership is to understand your own important needs and build on them.

You cannot be everything to everyone. Yes, it is good to understand each individual's needs and try to satisfy them, but for me the key is to focus on a few things and do those well. The easiest thing is to be good at what is important to you. In other words, treat others like you want to be treated yourself.

Trying to understand myself, I have come to the conclusion that there are four main things that keep me motivated.

1. There has to be a greater meaning in what I do.
2. I have to feel recognized for the things I do.
3. I have to feel trust and a sense of togetherness with the people I work with.
4. I have to feel that I develop and learn from what I am doing.

If all four criteria are fulfilled, I feel extremely motivated and energized in what I do.

In most jobs I have had within Ikea, I have had the privilege to work with people who have given me the opportunity to fulfill these needs. I do not think, however, that the responsibility lies only with the manager. To a considerable extent, I myself am responsible for making this happen, and my manger's role is to support me.

Let me elaborate on my four criteria.

A Meaning in What I Do

In every assignment I have had, I have started by getting a bearing on the overall purpose of what I or the organization I was responsible for should achieve. What are the long-term objectives? What are the strategies to achieve the objectives? And why is this the right path to take? I have always found it difficult to work unless I know where I am heading and why.

The most recent example is the 10-year direction "Ten Jobs in Ten Years" discussed previously. As I said earlier, together with putting the new team together, this was my first priority. In my experience, a clear direction that is understood and accepted creates a sense of security and stability for the organization, and it helps focus energy and resources. Creating meaning with a common direction or plan also means making it broad enough so that most people can see their roles and how they can contribute. Seeing the overall direction of the company and one's own role in this plan creates motivation. "Ten Jobs" was proof that this works. An even stronger example of the power of creating motivation with the meaning of work is the Ikea vision, "To create a better everyday life for the many people." In this case, the direction also has a social ambition. This is extremely powerful. This vision has been very motivating both for me and for many Ikea employees.

Feeling Recognized for What I Do

This is probably the greatest motivator of all. I would even go so far as to say that recognition is the most important driver of mankind—so important to get, but so difficult to satisfy. In all leadership evaluation I have seen within Ikea, the manager's ability to "give feedback on work performance" is always the question that gets the lowest score.

The need for recognition is endless. The more you get, the more you want. Recognition can take many forms. What has always mattered to me is to be given responsibility and independence, to be seen and heard and to be respected. Over the years, I have been told that I work like that with the people reporting to me. Yes, put demands on people. Yes, make them accountable. And yes, follow up, but give them the freedom to solve the task and find the solution themselves. Again, this is an example of treating others like I want to be treated myself.

Feeling Trust and a Sense of Togetherness with the People I Work With

A sense of belonging is a very basic need for most people. Look at the importance we give to family or our friends. When people leave a job or a company, you often hear that what they miss the most are the people and friendships, not the tasks they performed.

I experienced this myself when I was the country manager in the UK. When I arrived, there was a lot of mistrust between store managers and the managers of the central organization (service office). Making it a priority to build trust within that group, we tried to spend quality time together during four years. The relationships we developed during those years were key to the business success we experienced.

On a broader business scale, togetherness and trust can be supported with business actions such as creating common visions, objectives, priorities, and shared company values. In the case of Ikea, a strong shared vision and values create a strong sense of togetherness and motivation for many people. On an individual level, what is important to me to gain trust in others are traits such as being honest, being open and accessible, being straightforward, keeping my word, and setting high moral and ethical standards—characteristics I would hope others see in me.

To Feel that I Develop and Learn in My Job

This has certainly never been a problem during my 26 years with Ikea. Working in a growing global organization with tasks ranging from production to retail, combined with a company culture where you are encouraged to try out new ideas and take responsibility, there have always been plenty of opportunities to develop and learn. Having had the opportunity to take on big responsibilities at an early age, I have tried to provide the same chance to the people working with me.

In conclusion, what I have been striving for in my leadership is to create an environment where people feel welcome, motivated, and energized. Where they feel there is a meaning in work worthy of their best efforts. Where they feel recognized, respected, and a pride in what they are doing. Where they feel support and trust from their colleagues. And where they get the opportunity to develop themselves and the business.

The Power of Leadership

Promoting good leadership has always been important in Ikea. The company invests a considerable amount of time in leadership training. The idea was to always try to connect the leadership development with the Ikea values, to make sure the Ikea leadership is based on the Ikea values. And you can see the result of that quite clearly on the sales floor.

Humbleness, determination, togetherness, cost consciousness, common sense, lack of status, a willingness to give and take responsibility—all those traits that are used to describe the Ikea values I feel also apply to most Ikea leaders and employees. In the internal surveys, 70 percent of Ikea employees say that their manager is a good example of the Ikea values.

Conclusion

Doing Good Business while
Being a Good Business

have been discussing in the past few chapters primarily technical issues about how to structure and run an effective, profitable
business, one that provides a healthy, supportive working environment for its employees while at the same time fulfilling a social
vision of giving back to the community. In my conclusion, I want
to return to the question with which I opened this book: What
does it take to be a company that manages to both deliver a healthy
profit and contribute to a better society? My conclusions are related
primarily to the retail sector, but I would like to think that some of
these points are relevant also to other businesses.

For success, there are four main points:

- A vision with a social ambition and a strong value base
- Differentiation through control of the value chain
- Market leadership and a balanced market portfolio.
- Company control by a committed owner with a long-term
  perspective

A Vision with a Social Ambition
and a Strong Value Base

Building strong values and a vision with a social ambition will help
you improve not only the profitability but also help you gain respect
and trust among the society at large. You will be competitive in the

labor market, and you will be able to recruit, motivate, and retain the best people. As previously discussed, most people want more from work than just a paycheck. They want true meaning in what they do, and they want to work with people who share their values.

If you have the best people and they are motivated, business results will necessarily follow. A vision with a social ambition is key to making your commitment to be a good company credible. It is also important, in my opinion, that the core values of the company are not only customer related or efficiency related. They have to speak to what fundamentally motivates people, such as recognition and trust. These could be values such honesty, respect, equality, openness, and fairness. When you are truly committed to being a good company that contributes to a better society, profit will also come through more loyal customers. I know this is difficult to quantify, but in the long run I am confident it will pay off.

At the end of the day, if you run or own a company, what do you want to be known for? That you had the biggest house, the biggest yacht, the fattest bank account—or that you made a difference to many people? Recognition is our biggest driving force. Recognition will come to you when you work in a good company.

Differentiation through Control of the Value Chain

Differentiation in product range and price is key to superior profitability. When the product range is controlled by other companies—as is commonly the case in the fast-moving consumer goods sector (FMCG)—retail companies have a problem. Retail sectors where this is a dilemma include the food sector, the DIY sector, and the electronics sector. In these sectors, the range is pretty much the same among different retailers, and competing on price is almost impossible. The brand owners are interested in keeping stable prices, and the retailers have a hard time competing on price.

With purchasing prices in these sectors being more or less the same, any retail price reduction initiative will start a price war and only lead to lower margins for everyone. This is something most listed retailers avoid at any cost, since they must deliver results each quarter. Retailers may try in their promotions to look as if they have the lowest price, but in reality it is in everybody's interest to keep the real prices stable. Pricing strategy is limited to monitoring competition and reacting to what they do. This setup with two mutually dependent actors—the brand owners and the retailers—tends to result in a higher general price level for the customer.

Since the product range is the same and prices are the same, the most important point of difference is location. Service, store basic standards, customer financing, and staff competence are other customer benefits that are used by the retailers as differentiators. This, in my opinion, has marginal impact on driving sales and bottom line results compared to product range and price differentiation.

For companies like Ikea, which own the brand and control the supply chain, the potential for higher margins or lower sales prices or both probably accounts for a better margin of at least 10 percentage points. Look at the difference in profit between own brand retailers and no brand retailers and the profitability of the FMCGs, and you'll find support for this hypothesis.

Own brand retailers must focus on maximizing their advantage by optimizing product range development and the supply chain with a process-oriented setup.

No brand retailers have a much bigger challenge since they need to increase the level of own brands and ideally move to 100 percent. This is not just a matter of "fixing" some products. It means a total transformation of the company. Developing a strong brand— an own product range—is a very different competence compared to being a pure retailer. I cannot think of any company that has made the transformation fully and effectively. (Introducing some private labels is not what I mean; to get the full benefit, you need to move to a position like Ikea or H&M.)

Market Leadership and a Balanced Market Portfolio

When all other components are the same, size seems to make a difference to profitability. The statistics in the aforementioned sectors (food, DIY, and electronics) seem to confirm this.

Given similar product range and prices, the companies with the highest sales levels seem to outperform others in terms of profitability. You will get somewhat better purchase prices, and if you put operating procedures in place to achieve other scale benefits, you will have some cost advantages. For this reason, market leadership is important.

To leverage risk and prepare for future growth, successful retailers must also establish a healthy mix of mature markets and future growth markets. Doing this well while maintaining a high level of profitability seems to depend on a strong position in the home market, a willingness to take risks, and the competence to adapt the business model to different circumstances in countries with low purchasing power, less stable financial and political systems, and very different cultures and values. Not many big box retailers have been successful in doing this.

A Committed Owner with a Long-Term Perspective

From my experience at Ikea, I saw that a strong owner brought a lot of good things to the business such as a long-term perspective, a willingness to take risk, establishing a company heritage, a purpose and values, and an ability to check temptations toward exaggerated compensation. With their knowledge of the company, strong owners provide a relevant and healthy pressure to improve the business. Strong owners tend to hang around for a longer time than CEOs, and this is helpful to achieve continuity. All these traits are important to become a responsible, profitable business.

Is it possible to do these things in a listed (public) company with a weak or diluted ownership structure? The short-term focus in such companies is on profit, with potentially negative impacts on risk taking, long-term transformation ambitions, and establishing a heritage and a purpose other than profit. But with a strong board and strong management with the right values and vision who are committed for a longer time, I am hopeful it can be done.

Some Good Examples

Who are the companies that combine responsible business practices with high profitability? In the retail sector—looking at indicators such as profit, sales growth, various rankings in innovation, respected companies, attractive employers, brand recognition, etc.—companies such as Ikea, H&M, and Inditex are always well placed. All these companies live up to the criteria of differentiation in range and price, visions and values, strong owners with a long-term perspective, and market leadership.

Do you have to get to a point of high profitability before you start working on being a good company? I don't think so. Creating strong values and vision, long-term thinking, and other things will make you a profitable company. It is not something you tack on at the end.

Most companies are in very different situations in their life cycles. Some are in a survival mode, some are profitable, and some are both profitable and have a good reputation. I would count Ikea in that latter category, but very few if any have come all the way to establish a position as truly good corporate citizens.

The Next Steps

There is always one more step to take. If we look at Ikea, what else must it do to live up to the vision of "being for the majority of people"? The company has been able to reach the middle classes with its product range and prices. A good achievement, true, but the real challenge will be to provide well-designed and good-quality home furnishings for the really poor, be it in the villages of India or in the inner cities of Western countries.

In terms of equality within the company's workforce, yes, some improvements have undoubtedly happened regarding gender equality. The more challenging task of creating management opportunities for minority groups in the different markets of operations has so far been unsuccessful. In terms of environmental work, yes, a lot has been achieved, but some real challenges remain to be addressed both among suppliers and in the areas of energy and raw material use.

Contributing to less poverty, more equality, and a better environment are changing perspectives on the purpose of business. *Such fundamental questions cannot be solved by governments alone. I believe a bigger contribution from the business community is necessary.* This would also help bridge the lack of trust in business that we are increasingly witnessing.

A Duty to Grow

I think a company's purpose is to fulfill itself, to grow, and develop to the best it can be. Doing this means creating a better balance between financial accomplishments and doing the right thing. Doing the right thing, in my view, means that the company's reason for existence should be to contribute to a better society. Responsible companies have a duty to grow because their contribution to society is so important. In reality, this probably calls for more companies being controlled by strong owners with the right values and dedication. And if not that, the boards and management of public companies must be brave enough to work as if they owned the company—taking risks, putting value on vision, etc.

Is it naïve to believe that change can happen? After all, the drive for financial wealth is a strong motivator in the business community, and therefore contributing to a better society will never be a priority among the vast majority of company owners and managers. Adam Smith, in his epic work *The Wealth of Nations*, wrote, "It is not from the benevolence of the butcher, the brewer, or the baker that we expect our dinner, but from their regard to their own interest. We address ourselves, not to their humanity but to their self-love, and never talk to them of our own necessities but of their advantages."

For those who are motivated by profits and through profits by the creation of their own wealth, we must make the case that this objective is best achieved through being a good company because good companies attract good people who can then deliver the profits. For those who are motivated by the recognition of others (the vast majority, in my opinion) we must make the case that being a good company—doing good for others—will bring you vastly more recognition than merely being rich. And for some people, of course, this is simply the right thing to do.

I am hopeful that change can happen. Fifty years ago, the rich and powerful were the icons of society. Today they are still admired, but not for being merely rich but rather for how they conduct their business and what they do with their wealth. People like Ingvar Kamprad, Ratan Tata, Bill Gates, and the Google founders Sergey Brin and Larry Page are good examples of today's socially conscious businesspeople. *These* are the icons of business, not the managers of Wall Street.

The changing values in society, the good example set by great entrepreneurs, and the business case for profitability resulting from being a good company are all powerful reasons for change.

About the Author

Anders Dahlvig has a BA degree in business from Lund University, Sweden, and a MA degree in economics from UCSB. He worked for Ikea from 1983 to 2009, the last 10 years as president and CEO. He now holds several company board assignments including Kingfisher plc, HM AB, Oriflame SA, The New Wave Group, and Axel Johnson AB.